FINANCIAL FREEDOM FORMULA

KODHANDA RAMAKRISHNA VARRE

VV DURGA PRASAD VARRE

To my beloved parents,

Your love, sacrifices, and unwavering support have shaped the person we are today. You taught us the value of hard work, integrity, and perseverance—lessons that extend far beyond money but form the foundation of true wealth in life.

This book is a tribute to you, for every lesson you instilled in me and for being my greatest inspiration.

With endless gratitude and love,

CMA V K Ramakrishna
VV Durga Prasad Varre

Contents

Preface

Money plays a crucial role in our lives, yet financial literacy remains one of the most overlooked aspects of education. Many individuals spend decades earning money but fail to understand how to manage, grow, and sustain it. This book, *Financial Freedom Formula*, is a humble attempt to bridge that gap by presenting timeless financial wisdom through a compelling, relatable story.

The inspiration behind this book stems from real-life experiences of ours and countless individuals who have struggled with financial decisions. We have seen people work tirelessly, only to remain trapped in financial stress due to poor money management. On the other hand, we have also observed those who, despite earning modest incomes, build sustainable wealth by making the right financial choices.

Financial Freedom Formula is not just another personal finance book filled with theories and numbers. Instead, it takes you on a journey through the life of Arjun, a middle-class professional who, like many, is caught in the cycle of earning and spending with little thought about his financial future. Through the mentorship of Eshwar, he learns the principles of wealth creation, financial independence, and the true meaning of financial freedom. Each chapter unfolds valuable lessons, making financial planning easy to understand, engaging, and most importantly, practical.

What sets this book apart is its storytelling approach. Rather than presenting financial concepts in a textbook format, we have woven them into an emotional and thought-provoking narrative. Readers will find themselves relating to Arjun's struggles, triumphs, and ultimate transformation. Whether you are just starting your financial journey or looking to refine your investment strategy, this book will provide you with actionable insights that can change your financial future.

Our goal is simple: To empower you with the knowledge and mindset needed to take control of your finances and live a life of abundance and security. If this book helps even one reader break free from financial stress and build a prosperous future, our mission will be fulfilled.

We invite you to embark on this journey with Arjun and discover the path to true financial freedom.

Happy reading!

CMA V K Ramakrishna

VV Durgaprasad Varre

Acknowledgements

Writing this book has been an incredible journey, and I am deeply grateful to the people who have played a significant role in making it possible.

First and foremost, I express my heartfelt gratitude to **my parents** for their unconditional love, sacrifices, and the values they have instilled in me. Their support has been the foundation of everything I have achieved in life.

A special thanks to **my brother and co-author**, who has been an integral part of this journey. His insights, collaboration, and unwavering encouragement have been invaluable in shaping this book into what it is today.

To **my wife**, whose patience, understanding, and constant support have given me the strength to dedicate myself to this project—I am forever grateful. Her belief in me and my vision has been my greatest motivation.

I also extend my deepest gratitude to my real-life mentors, **Shri D. Zitendra Rao Garu** and **Shri B. Ramesh Kumar Garu**. Their wisdom, guidance, and teachings have profoundly influenced my understanding of financial wisdom and life itself. Their mentorship has been a beacon of knowledge that I will always cherish.

Finally, to every reader of this book—thank you for allowing me to be a part of your financial journey. May this book help you achieve financial freedom and create a prosperous future for yourself and your loved ones.

With deep appreciation,
CMA V K Ramakrishna

Prologue

Arjun sat by the window, sipping his morning coffee, as the city outside bustled with people rushing to work. He used to be one of them—trapped in the endless cycle of earning, spending, and barely saving. He had done everything society told him: studied hard, got a stable job, and climbed the corporate ladder. Yet, financial security always felt like an illusion—one unexpected expense could shake his world.

Then, everything changed.

A chance meeting with Eshwar, a man who seemed to have unlocked the secret to financial independence, set him on a journey that transformed his life. Through failures, realizations, and hard-earned wisdom, Arjun discovered that financial freedom was not just about having more money—it was about having choices. It was about living life on his own terms, without fear or uncertainty.

This book is not just Arjun's story—it is the story of millions who dream of escaping the paycheck-to-paycheck trap, of breaking free from financial stress, and of achieving true wealth.

Are you ready to rewrite your financial future? The journey begins now.

CHAPTER ONE

The Illusion of Wealth

1. Arjun's Comfortable Yet Stressful Life

The sun peeked through the beige curtains of Arjun's high-rise apartment, casting soft streaks of light across the neatly arranged bedroom. The sound of the alarm on his phone jolted him awake. With a sigh, he reached out and tapped the screen, silencing the persistent chime. It was 6:30 AM—another weekday, another long day at work.

Arjun pushed aside the silk duvet and swung his legs over the edge of the bed. His wife, Suneetha, stirred beside him, mumbling something about waking up in five more minutes. He smiled faintly. They had been married for nearly eight years now. Their life together was comfortable—at least on the surface.

His apartment, located in one of Hyderabad's premium gated communities, had been his dream home. A sprawling 3BHK with a balcony overlooking the city, complete with modern interiors and sleek furniture. Outside, his recently purchased SUV stood gleaming in the parking lot, a testament to his success. His colleagues often admired his lifestyle—the weekend brunches at fancy restaurants, the vacations in Goa or Kerala, the expensive gifts he bought for Suneetha on special occasions.

Yet, beneath the polished exterior, Arjun was drowning in financial stress.

As he stepped into the shower, his mind was already racing—project deadlines, performance reviews, and the unending financial pressures he had grown used to. The home loan EMI of ₹65,000 was due next week, the credit card bill had crossed ₹1 lakh again, and Suneetha had mentioned something about an upcoming family function where they would have to buy expensive gifts.

Every month was the same. The salary would get credited, and within days, most of it would vanish into loan repayments, bills, and daily expenses. Despite earning a handsome ₹2 lakh per month, they barely saved anything.

"Maybe I just need to earn more," he muttered to himself as he adjusted his tie in the mirror.

It was a thought he had repeated to himself for years. A salary hike, a promotion, or a side hustle—one of these would eventually solve his problems. Wouldn't it?

As he stepped out of his apartment and walked toward his SUV, the question lingered in his mind, heavier than ever.

His life looked perfect on the outside—a high-paying job, a stylish apartment in a gated community, and a recently purchased SUV that gleamed under the morning sun. Yet, beneath the surface, an unsettling feeling gnawed at him. No matter how much he earned, it never seemed enough.

Locking the car door, he glanced around the parking lot. A few months ago, when he had bought his SUV, he had felt a rush of pride. But today, standing beside it, he felt something else—an unease he couldn't quite place.

As he settled into the driver's seat and turned the ignition, his mind wandered back to last night's conversation with Suneetha.

"Arjun, have you noticed how we're always waiting for the next salary just to clear the previous month's expenses?" she had asked, her voice filled with concern. "It feels like we're earning just to keep up, not to get ahead."

He had brushed it off then, saying it was just a phase. But now, as he stared at the traffic ahead, her words echoed in his mind.

Just then, his phone vibrated on the dashboard. A notification flashed on the screen—a message from Sumant.

"Bro, check this out! Just arrived in Dubai. Dinner at Burj Al Arab tonight. Life's good! "

Attached was a picture of Sumant, dressed in a crisp white linen shirt and sunglasses, standing next to a Lamborghini. The towering skyline of Dubai gleamed in the background, a picture of opulence and extravagance.

2. The Comparison Trap: Sumant's Lavish Lifestyle

Arjun let out a deep sigh. This was nothing new. Every few months, Sumant would be off to another exotic location—Europe, Bali, Singapore, or the Maldives. His Instagram feed was a never-ending stream of luxurious vacations, expensive watches, high-end cars, and VIP experiences.

And it wasn't just the travel. Sumant always had the latest gadgets—whether it was the newest iPhone, a top-of-the-line MacBook, or the most advanced noise-cancelling headphones. The guy never seemed to worry about money.

Arjun couldn't help but feel a twinge of jealousy. They had started their careers around the same time, working at similar corporate jobs. Yet, while Arjun carefully planned his expenses and still struggled to save, Sumant lived like a king, spending freely without a care in the world.

A few days ago, they had met for dinner at a five-star hotel's rooftop lounge. Arjun had hesitated before ordering, mentally calculating how much the bill might come to. Meanwhile, Sumant had ordered premium whiskey, rare sushi, and a gourmet steak without even glancing at the menu.

"Dude, why do you stress so much about money?" Sumant had laughed, sipping his drink. "What's the point of earning if you don't enjoy life? Work hard, play harder!"

That line had stuck with Arjun. May be Sumant was right. Maybe he was overthinking things. After all, what was the point of all those late nights at work, the stress, and the hard-earned money if he wasn't enjoying it?

Still, something didn't sit right. How was Sumant affording this lifestyle? His salary couldn't be that much higher than Arjun's.

Just then, a sharp honk from behind snapped him out of his thoughts. The traffic light had turned green. He quickly accelerated, but his mind remained tangled in comparison.

Was he missing something? Or was he simply not earning enough to truly enjoy life the way Sumant did?

The question gnawed at him as he drove toward his office, unaware that he was about to face a financial reality check that would change everything.

3. The Harsh Reality Check

Arjun pulled into the office parking lot, still lost in thought. The morning had been like any other—coffee in hand, mind buzzing with emails and deadlines—but a lingering discomfort sat in the back of his mind. As he stepped out of his SUV, his phone rang. It was Suneetha.

There was an urgency in her voice that made his stomach tighten.

"Arjun, it's Papa... He suddenly collapsed. We're rushing him to the hospital."

His heart pounded. "What happened?"

"We don't know yet. The doctor said they need to run tests immediately."

Arjun didn't wait to respond. He turned, got back into his car, and sped toward the hospital, his hands gripping the steering wheel tighter than ever.

By the time he reached the emergency ward, Suneetha was pacing outside. Her face was pale, eyes red-rimmed.

"Doctor?" Arjun asked breathlessly.

"They're running tests," she said, trying to hold back her tears. "They need an advance payment of ₹2 lakh before proceeding with further treatment."

The words hit him like a punch to the gut. Two lakhs?

Arjun instinctively reached for his phone, checking his bank balance. The numbers on the screen made his chest tighten further. Between his home loan EMI, credit card dues, and monthly expenses, his savings were next to nothing.

A cold realization settled over him.

For all the years he had worked, for all the money he had earned, he didn't have enough in his account to handle one medical emergency.

The receptionist cleared her throat, breaking his thoughts. "Sir, we need the payment to proceed."

His mind raced. There was no time to think. He did what seemed like the only option—he pulled out his credit card and swiped.

A temporary solution. A decision that carried a burden he hadn't yet fully realized.

As he sat in the waiting area, staring at the payment receipt in his hand, another thought crept into his mind—one that sent a chill down his spine.

If this had happened a few days later, after his credit card bill was due, what would he have done?

The stress of debt, of living paycheck to paycheck, of never having an emergency fund—it all came crashing down on him in that moment.

For the first time in his life, Arjun felt truly vulnerable.

4. Questioning the Definition of Wealth

Arjun sat in the dimly lit hospital corridor, his elbows resting on his knees, fingers tightly interlocked. The steady hum of the overhead lights and the occasional sound of nurses walking by filled the silence. His father-in-law was stable now, but the weight of the situation pressed down on him like never before.

His eyes drifted to the payment receipt in his hand—₹2 lakh, charged to his credit card. He knew what that meant. A massive bill next month, interest piling up if he couldn't pay in full, and another cycle of financial strain.

For the first time, a question he had never dared to ask himself echoed in his mind.

"If I'm earning so much, why do I feel so financially insecure?"

It wasn't as if he was unemployed or struggling. His salary was well above average, he lived in a premium apartment, drove a high-end SUV, and dined at expensive restaurants. But today, none of those things had helped him. When he had needed money the most, he hadn't had it.

His entire financial life suddenly seemed like an illusion—a grand performance where he played the role of a successful man, yet behind the scenes, he was drowning.

Lost in thought, he barely noticed Suneetha sitting down beside him.

She let out a sigh, her voice barely above a whisper. "It's exhausting, isn't it?"

He turned to her, surprised. "What do you mean?"

She ran her fingers through her hair, looking straight ahead. "This constant struggle. No matter how much we earn, it never feels like enough. One emergency, and we're already at the edge."

Arjun exhaled deeply. "I was just thinking the same thing. How did we end up here? We both have good jobs, we make more than most people... and yet, I had to swipe my credit card for an emergency."

She gave a bitter chuckle. "You know what's worse? I've been feeling this way for a long time. I just didn't say it out loud. Every month, I see our bank balance drain away—EMIs, bills, credit card payments, expenses. We never really save. We just earn, spend, and repeat."

Her words struck him harder than he expected.

"I thought earning more would fix everything," Arjun admitted. "I kept believing that once I got a better salary, a promotion, or a bigger bonus, we'd finally be secure. But no matter how much we make, it just disappears."

Suneetha looked at him, eyes tired but filled with unspoken fears. "It's not just about earning, is it?"

Arjun shook his head. "No... it's not."

For years, he had believed that wealth was about income, about having a high-paying job and affording the best things. But today, as he sat in that hospital, burdened by debt and uncertainty, he realized how flawed that belief was.

He didn't need to earn more. He needed to understand money better.

And for the first time, he felt a desperate need to change—to break free from this endless cycle of financial stress.

This moment, sitting next to Suneetha in the dim hospital corridor, marked the beginning of something new.

A search for true financial freedom.

******

Key Takeaways from Chapter 1: The Illusion of Wealth

1. Income Does Not Equal Wealth

- Earning a high salary does not guarantee financial security.
- Without proper money management, even a good income can lead to financial stress.

2. The Comparison Trap Leads to Financial Instability

- Comparing your lifestyle with others can push you into unnecessary spending.
- Just because someone appears wealthy doesn't mean they are financially stable.

3. The Importance of an Emergency Fund

- Unexpected expenses can arise anytime—having a financial cushion prevents reliance on credit.
- Credit card debt is expensive due to high interest rates, making emergencies worse if not planned for.

4. Recognizing Financial Illusions

- Wealth is not about how much you earn but how well you manage your money.
- Owning luxury items does not mean financial freedom—true wealth is about financial stability.

5. The Need for a Mindset Shift

- More income won't solve financial problems if spending habits don't change.
- Financial freedom starts with understanding how money works, not just earning more.

These realizations push Arjun to seek better financial knowledge, setting the stage for his journey toward financial independence.

CHAPTER TWO

Meeting the Mentor

Frustration and Seeking Answers

Arjun sat on the balcony of his apartment, staring at the flickering city lights. The sound of honking cars and distant chatter filled the air, but his mind was lost in a whirlwind of numbers—EMIs, credit card bills, grocery expenses, school fees. It had been two weeks since the hospital incident, and the weight of financial insecurity still sat heavy on his chest.

He had always assumed that earning a high salary meant financial stability. Yet, here he was—constantly worried about the next expense, the next bill, the next crisis. The illusion of control he once had over his money was crumbling.

In search of answers, he turned to the internet. Late into the night, he scrolled through finance blogs and YouTube videos. Some advised aggressive stock investments, others swore by mutual funds, while some pushed extreme frugality. The conflicting advice only added to his confusion.

"Maybe I should start a side hustle?" he wondered, clicking on an article about passive income. But even that required time, energy, and—ironically—money to get started. Frustration mounted as he realized that none of

these so-called solutions addressed his real problem: why was he earning so much yet feeling broke?

Just as he was about to shut his laptop, a familiar name appeared on his screen. It was a social media post from Eshwar, his old college mentor. The caption read: *Financial Independence: The Freedom You Deserve.*

Arjun hesitated. He hadn't spoken to Eshwar in years. Back in college, Eshwar was the one person he looked up to for advice—wise, pragmatic, and always a step ahead. He remembered how, years ago, Eshwar had quit his high-paying corporate job, saying he wanted to 'work for himself.' Arjun had thought he was crazy back then. But now, curiosity stirred within him.

Without overthinking, he clicked on Eshwar's profile and typed a message:

"Hey Eshwar! Long time. Saw your post on financial independence. Would love to catch up!"

He hit send, unaware that this small decision would change his life forever.

Reuniting with Eshwar

The next morning, Arjun woke up to a notification.

"Hey Arjun! It's been ages. Glad to hear from you. Let's catch up. How about Café Serene at 6 PM today?"

Arjun smiled. Café Serene. The place where they used to sit for hours discussing career aspirations, business ideas, and life plans. It had been years since he last visited.

After wrapping up his work, he drove to the café, his mind buzzing with questions. Would Eshwar even remember their old conversations? Had he really cracked the financial code, or was it just another social media gimmick?

As he walked in, the aroma of freshly brewed coffee filled the air. And there he was—Eshwar, sitting by the window, sipping tea.

At first glance, he looked the same. But there was something different about him. He carried himself with a calm confidence, a quiet ease that Arjun couldn't quite place. No designer watch, no fancy car keys on the table—just a simple kurta, a warm smile, and an aura of contentment.

"Arjun! Look at you, man. It's been what—ten years?" Eshwar stood up, giving him a firm handshake.

"Yeah, a decade already," Arjun chuckled, taking a seat. "You haven't changed much, but I must say, you look... different."

Eshwar laughed. "Different? In a good way, I hope?"

Arjun nodded. "You look at peace. And I don't mean just relaxed—I mean, really at peace."

Eshwar leaned back, his eyes twinkling. "That's because I am. But tell me about you. How's life treating you?"

Arjun hesitated for a moment before sighing. "Honestly? It's stressful. I'm making more money than I ever have, but somehow, it never seems enough. The hospital incident last week was a wake-up call. I realized I'm just one emergency away from financial disaster. It's frustrating, Eshwar. I feel like I'm running on a treadmill—working hard but never moving forward."

Eshwar listened intently, nodding. "I know exactly how that feels. I was in your shoes once."

Arjun raised an eyebrow. "You? Come on, you've always been the guy who had everything figured out."

Eshwar smiled. "Not at all. I made the same mistakes, chased the same illusions of wealth. But one day, I realized something that changed everything."

Arjun leaned in. "And what was that?"

Eshwar took a slow sip of his tea before setting down the cup. "Let me ask you something, Arjun. If you lost your job today, how long could you survive without income?"

The question hit Arjun like a ton of bricks.

He did some quick mental calculations. Between his savings, credit card bills, and monthly expenses, the answer was painfully clear.

"...A month. Maybe two, if I cut back on a few things."

Eshwar nodded, as if he had expected that answer. "That, my friend, is the real measure of wealth. Not your salary, not your car, not your job title. The real question is—how long can you sustain your life without working?"

Arjun sat back, his mind spinning. He had never thought about wealth this way.

For the first time in his life, he realized—he wasn't rich. He was just a high-income earner living paycheck to paycheck.

The First Eye-Opening Question

Arjun stared at Eshwar, his mind racing. *How long could I survive without a paycheck?* It was such a simple question, yet it had never crossed his mind before.

"I always thought wealth was about how much you earn," Arjun admitted. "But if I can't survive more than a month without my salary, then... am I really wealthy?"

Eshwar smiled knowingly. "Exactly. Most people confuse a high income with financial security. But true wealth isn't about how much you make—it's about how much you keep and how long it can sustain you."

Arjun leaned forward. "So, what's the magic number? How long should someone be able to survive without a paycheck?"

Eshwar took a thoughtful sip of his tea. "It depends on your goals. But at the very least, you should have enough to survive for six months to a year without worrying. And beyond that, the real goal is financial independence—where your money works for you, not the other way around."

Arjun frowned. "That sounds... impossible. My expenses take up most of my salary. Between EMIs, bills, and daily expenses, saving even a small amount feels difficult."

Eshwar chuckled. "You're not alone. That's exactly how I felt when I started. But tell me, Arjun—do you know where every rupee of your salary goes?"

Arjun hesitated. "Roughly, yes. I mean, I pay my loans, rent, bills, and then whatever's left is spent on groceries, shopping, and maybe a trip now and then."

Eshwar raised an eyebrow. "And how much do you save each month?"

Arjun scratched his head. "It... depends. Some months, I save a little. Other months, unexpected expenses wipe out my savings."

Eshwar smiled. "That's what I thought. You're not alone, Arjun. Most people have no idea where their money is actually going. They earn, spend, and hope for the best. But here's the thing—hope is not a financial strategy."

Arjun nodded slowly. He had always assumed that making more money was the solution. But here was Eshwar, living proof that financial freedom wasn't about earning more—it was about managing what you already had.

Eshwar placed his cup down and looked Arjun in the eye. "If you really want to take control of your finances, start with one simple step: track your expenses. Every single rupee. For one month. Then, come back and tell me what you learned."

Arjun frowned. "Track every rupee? That sounds tedious."

Eshwar chuckled. "That's what I thought too, until I did it. Trust me, Arjun, awareness is the first step to financial freedom. Do this, and I guarantee you'll see money differently."

Arjun sighed, then nodded. "Fine. One month. I'll track every rupee."

As he walked out of the café, he felt something he hadn't felt in a long time—hope. Maybe, just maybe, he was about to change his life.

The Concept of Financial Freedom

The cool evening breeze brushed against Arjun's face as he walked toward his car. His mind was buzzing with thoughts. *If you lost your job today, how long could you survive?* The question refused to leave him.

As he drove home, he kept replaying his conversation with Eshwar. *Financial freedom? Money working for me instead of me working for money?* The idea sounded appealing, but also... unrealistic.

That night, after dinner, Arjun sat on the balcony with a cup of tea. Suneetha noticed his silence. "You look lost in thought," she said, sitting beside him.

"I met Eshwar today," Arjun said, still staring into the distance.

Suneetha smiled. "Your college mentor? It's been years! How is he?"

"He's doing great. He's financially independent now—doesn't work for money anymore. He only works because he enjoys it."

Suneetha's eyebrows lifted. "That sounds like a dream."

Arjun nodded. "Yeah. And the way he explained it, financial freedom isn't just for billionaires. It's about having enough assets that generate income, so we don't have to depend on a paycheck."

Suneetha leaned forward. "Like passive income?"

"Exactly," Arjun said. "He told me that financial security isn't about how much we earn, but how long we can sustain ourselves without working. And right now, if I lose my job, we won't last beyond a month."

Suneetha's smile faded. She had never thought about it that way. "That's... scary," she admitted.

Arjun took a deep breath. "Eshwar wasn't always financially free. He was like us—living paycheck to paycheck. Then, he realized that money should be a tool, not a trap. He started saving, investing, and building assets."

Suneetha thought for a moment. "We've always assumed that if we just earn more, things will get better. But no matter how much we earn, we still struggle."

"That's what hit me too," Arjun said. "Eshwar told me that lifestyle inflation keeps people stuck. When we earn more, we spend more—bigger house, better car, fancier vacations. But we never actually buy freedom."

Suneetha sighed. "So, what do we do?"

Arjun looked at her. "He gave me a challenge—to track our expenses for a month. Every rupee."

Suneetha raised an eyebrow. "That sounds exhausting."

Arjun chuckled. "That's what I said. But he believes awareness is the first step. If we don't know where our money is going, how can we ever control it?"

Suneetha thought for a moment. "Alright. Let's do it. One month."

As they sat there, Arjun felt something shift inside him. For the first time, he wasn't just worrying about money—he was taking action.

This wasn't just about making ends meet anymore.

It was about breaking free.

The Challenge

The next morning, Arjun sat at his desk, staring at a blank spreadsheet on his laptop. *Track every expense for a month.* It sounded simple, yet as he thought about it, he realized how little he actually knew about where their money went.

Suneetha walked in with a cup of coffee. "So, have you started?" she asked, peeking at the screen.

Arjun sighed. "I don't even know where to begin. I mean, I know our major expenses—EMIs, rent, utilities. But what about the smaller ones? The coffee breaks, impulse buys, random online orders?"

Suneetha smirked. "You mean like the ₹300 coffee you had with Sumant last week?"

Arjun chuckled. "Exactly. Those little things add up."

Suneetha sat beside him. "Alright, let's list out our fixed expenses first—things we pay every month no matter what."

Together, they started filling in the obvious numbers:

- **Home Loan EMI:** ₹35,000
- **Car Loan EMI:** ₹12,000
- **Credit Card Bills:** ₹8,000
- **Electricity, Internet, and Phone Bills:** ₹5,500
- **Groceries:** ₹10,000

As they added more, the total kept growing. By the time they were done, their fixed monthly expenses stood at **₹90,000.**

"That's already most of our salary," Arjun muttered. "And we haven't even added discretionary spending—dining out, shopping, entertainment."

Suneetha tapped her chin. "We should track every rupee we spend for a month. Just write it down as soon as we spend it."

Arjun hesitated. "You mean, every single expense?"

"Yes," she said firmly. "That's the only way we'll see the truth."

Arjun sighed but nodded. He created a shared note on his phone so they could both update it in real-time.

Week 1: Reality Hits

By the end of the first week, they sat down to review their expenses.

- **Coffee shops & snacks: ₹2,800**
- **Online shopping: ₹5,500**
- **Dining out: ₹4,200**
- **Entertainment (movies, subscriptions): ₹3,000**
- **Miscellaneous (random expenses): ₹3,500**

Arjun's eyes widened. "That's ₹19,000... in one week?"

Suneetha bit her lip. "And that's *after* paying our fixed expenses."

A realization dawned upon them—**they weren't just spending money; they were leaking money.**

Week 2: The Emotional Spending Trap

The second week, Arjun found himself hesitating before every purchase.

One evening, after a long day at work, he felt exhausted. His first instinct was to order food online, but he stopped. *Do I really need this, or am I just tired?*

Similarly, Suneetha noticed how often she added things to her online shopping cart out of boredom.

"Most of our spending isn't even intentional," she admitted. "It's just... habit."

They started questioning each purchase, and something strange happened—their unnecessary expenses **dropped by 40%** without even trying too hard.

Week 4: The Truth About Their Money

By the end of the month, they sat down with their tracked expenses. The numbers were clear:

- They were **spending nearly ₹25,000 a month on discretionary expenses**, most of which they couldn't even remember.
- Their total expenses were **pushing them dangerously close to their income limit every month**—leaving no room for savings.
- If they continued this way, financial freedom was impossible.

Arjun exhaled deeply. "We earn well, but we're spending like we have an unlimited supply."

Suneetha nodded. "No wonder we're always stressed about money. We've been earning for survival, not for freedom."

At that moment, Arjun knew—**this challenge wasn't just about tracking expenses. It was about taking control.**

With these insights in hand, he was ready to meet Eshwar again.

This time, he wasn't just looking for answers. He was ready to change.

*****

Key Takeaways from Chapter 2

1. Financial Stress Comes from Lack of Awareness

- Arjun realizes that despite his good income, he has no financial clarity.
- Most people assume earning more will solve their problems, but without control over expenses, money disappears unnoticed.

2. True Wealth is Not About Income—It's About Sustainability

- Eshwar challenges Arjun with a crucial question: *"If you lost your job today, how long could you survive?"*
- Arjun realizes he has no savings, making him financially fragile despite his high salary.
- Wealth is measured by how long you can maintain your lifestyle without active income.

3. The First Step to Financial Freedom is Awareness

- Tracking every rupee spent gives a true picture of financial habits.
- Arjun and Suneetha discover that a significant portion of their expenses are unnecessary and mindless.
- Small, unconscious spending habits add up to massive financial leaks.

4. Emotional Spending is a Hidden Trap

- Many expenses are driven by mood, convenience, or habit rather than real need.
- Ordering food, impulsive shopping, and entertainment spending often serve as stress relief.
- Once spending becomes intentional, unnecessary expenses automatically reduce.

5. Financial Independence is a Process, Not an Instant Change

- Eshwar's story proves that financial freedom isn't about drastic measures—it's about small, consistent actions over time.
- Arjun learns that it's never too late to start, but the sooner he takes control, the better his future will be.

6. The Challenge: The First Action Toward Change

- Arjun accepts Eshwar's challenge to track expenses for a month.
- This simple exercise is the turning point—it forces him to confront the truth about his financial habits.
- Awareness leads to action, and action leads to transformation.

This chapter lays the foundation for Arjun's journey toward financial independence.

The next step? Learning how to break free from the paycheck-to-paycheck cycle. ?

CHAPTER THREE

The Trap of Life Style Inflation

The Illusion of Progress

A week had passed since Arjun's conversation with Eshwar, and his mind was still preoccupied with the question that had shaken him to the core: *How long could he survive without income?* He had never thought about it before, but now, he couldn't ignore it.

Determined to find answers, he had started tracking his expenses, just as Eshwar had suggested. At first, it felt tedious—every rupee spent on coffee, subscriptions, dining out, or online shopping had to be noted down. But as the days went by, something shocking emerged: money was slipping through his fingers faster than he realized.

Sitting at his desk late at night, Arjun reviewed his expense list for the week. His jaw tightened.

- ₹4,000 on food delivery.
- ₹1,200 on a new smartwatch band he didn't really need.
- ₹2,500 for premium OTT subscriptions, half of which he barely used.
- ₹8,000 spent on weekend outings and casual shopping.

And the list went on.

No wonder I feel broke by the end of the month, he thought. Every time his salary increased, so did his expenses. He had always believed that earning more would solve his financial struggles, but reality was proving otherwise. The more he earned, the more he spent—without a second thought.

Looking back, he realized this pattern had followed him for years. When he had started his career with a ₹30,000 salary, he had managed just fine. But as his salary grew, so did his lifestyle. From upgrading his phone every year to dining at expensive restaurants, his definition of "necessities" had expanded.

But was he actually progressing? Or was he just running in circles, mistaking lifestyle upgrades for financial success?

That night, as Arjun stared at his financial reality laid bare on the screen, a deep realization sank in—he wasn't earning to build wealth; he was earning just to sustain an ever-growing lifestyle.

And if he didn't change something soon, he would remain trapped in this cycle forever.

Sumant's Overspending Mindset

A few days later, Arjun found himself sitting across from Sumant at their favorite café, a high-end spot tucked away in a bustling mall. The aroma of freshly brewed coffee filled the air, blending with the chatter of well-dressed professionals and influencers capturing aesthetic pictures of their lattes. Arjun had always loved these meetings with Sumant, but today, he had come with a different mindset.

As soon as Sumant arrived, he placed a sleek black box on the table with a satisfied grin. "Guess what I got?"

Before Arjun could respond, Sumant flipped open the box to reveal the latest premium smartwatch. Its glossy screen lit up as Sumant proudly tapped on it. "This thing can track my sleep, measure my ECG, and even predict my stress levels!"

Arjun raised an eyebrow. "Didn't you just buy a smartwatch last year?"

"Yeah, but that was outdated. This one has AI integration and a titanium build!" Sumant flexed his wrist to show it off. "Tech moves fast, man. You gotta keep up."

Arjun forced a smile, but inside, a thought lingered—was this really necessary? He had just started tracking his expenses and was shocked at how much he had been spending on things he never even noticed. And yet, here was Sumant, happily upgrading gadgets like changing clothes.

Their conversation soon shifted to their lives. Sumant, as always, had plenty to share.

"I just moved to a new place—one of those ultra-modern apartments with a rooftop pool. You should see the view at night! Sure, the rent is a little high, but totally worth it."

Arjun leaned in. "How much is your rent?"

"Just sixty grand a month," Sumant said casually, stirring his coffee.

Arjun nearly choked on his espresso. "Sixty thousand? That's more than half of what most people earn in a month!"

Sumant laughed. "Come on, man, we're not most people. We work hard, we earn well, so we should live well! What's the point of money if you don't spend it?"

Arjun hesitated before speaking. "I get that, but... don't you ever feel like you're just running in circles? You earn more, but you also spend more. Do you actually save anything?"

Sumant waved his hand dismissively. "Dude, saving is overrated. As long as I keep making more, I'm fine. If I ever need money, there's always credit cards. I pay the minimum due, and life goes on."

Arjun sat back, his mind racing. For years, he had admired Sumant's lifestyle—the fancy dinners, luxury vacations, top-of-the-line gadgets. He had assumed that Sumant had everything figured out. But now, for the first time, he saw things differently.

"You know," Sumant continued, "I just leased a new car. You should see it—a beauty on wheels. The showroom guy told me leasing is smarter than buying because I can upgrade to a new model every few years. So, why get stuck with the same old car for years?"

Arjun frowned. "But... after all those payments, do you ever own the car?"

Sumant shrugged. "Who cares? Ownership is old-fashioned. Everything is about experiences now. The world is changing, man. Money isn't meant to sit in a bank, it's meant to be used!"

Arjun felt a strange discomfort. He had always believed that a bigger paycheck meant a better life. Sumant's words had once been his own. But after his conversation with Eshwar, something inside him had shifted.

For the first time, he questioned whether Sumant was truly wealthy—or just playing the part.

"Sumant," Arjun said slowly, choosing his words carefully, "What if one day... you stop making more?"

Sumant chuckled. "That'll never happen. There's always a way to make money. And besides, that's why we work—to make sure that day never comes!"

Arjun nodded, but deep down, a realization settled in. Sumant wasn't financially free. He was just another hamster on a faster wheel.

And for the first time in his life, Arjun wasn't sure if he wanted to be on that wheel anymore.

Sumant laughed. "Savings? Who needs savings when you have a steady paycheck?" He leaned back, sipping his coffee. "The way I see it, there's always more money to be made. And if I ever need extra, I have my credit cards."

Arjun didn't respond. He realized that Sumant was trapped in a different way—chasing an ever-expanding lifestyle, convinced that more money would always come.

For years, Arjun had admired Sumant's lifestyle. But today, for the first time, he wasn't sure if he envied it anymore.

Eshwar's Lesson on Lifestyle Inflation

The week had been a whirlwind for Arjun. Since tracking his expenses, he had been forced to confront some uncomfortable truths about his financial habits. Every evening, he would sit at his desk, staring at his notepad filled with figures—swiping through past transactions on his banking app, highlighting amounts that had seemed insignificant at the time but had piled up alarmingly over the months.

It wasn't just a few indulgences here and there. It was a pattern.

The extra-large pizza when a medium would have sufficed. The branded sneakers purchased on impulse, despite already having three pairs. The streaming services, each billed separately, adding up to thousands in subscriptions. The frequent coffee shop visits that made his office breaks enjoyable but had drained an unexpected portion of his salary.

He was earning more than he had five years ago—nearly double, in fact. And yet, his bank balance didn't reflect it. His savings were negligible, and if an emergency arose, he had no cushion to fall back on.

This realization gnawed at him.

By the time Sunday rolled around, he decided he needed to speak to Eshwar.

He called his mentor, and as expected, Eshwar agreed to meet him. They met at a quiet, modest café—not the kind Sumant would have chosen, but one where conversations flowed without the distractions of loud music or pretentious menus.

Eshwar greeted him warmly. "So, how's the expense tracking going?"

Arjun let out a deep sigh. "Eye-opening. And terrifying."

Eshwar chuckled. "Good. That means you're paying attention."

Arjun pulled out his notebook and flipped through the pages, tapping on the highlighted figures. "I always thought I was managing money well. But I see now that every time I got a salary hike, my expenses went up just as fast—sometimes even faster. I'm earning more, but I'm not saving more."

Eshwar nodded knowingly. "That, my friend, is **Lifestyle Inflation**."

Arjun frowned. "I've heard the term before, but I never really thought it applied to me."

Eshwar leaned forward. "That's the problem. Most people don't think it applies to them. They assume financial struggles happen only to those who earn less. But lifestyle inflation doesn't care about your income. It traps middle-class professionals, high-earning executives, even celebrities. It's why people who make lakhs a month can still be broke."

Arjun folded his arms. "But what causes it? Why do we keep increasing our expenses?"

Eshwar smiled. "Because we believe more money equals a better life. The moment we get a raise, we feel we 'deserve' an upgrade—a bigger house, a nicer car, the latest phone. We justify these choices as rewards for our hard work. But in reality, we are locking ourselves into a cycle where we must work harder just to maintain an ever-expanding lifestyle."

Arjun thought of Sumant's words: *Money isn't meant to sit in a bank; it's meant to be used.*

"But isn't spending a natural part of life?" Arjun asked. "What's wrong with enjoying the things we can afford?"

"Nothing is wrong with enjoying your earnings," Eshwar said. "The problem arises when your spending leaves you with no security. When you rely on the next paycheck to cover your increasing expenses, you aren't financially free—you're financially trapped."

He paused before continuing. "Let me give you an example. Imagine two people. The first earns ₹50,000 a month and saves ₹10,000. The second earns ₹ 1,00,000 but saves nothing. Who is wealthier?"

Arjun shrugged. "On paper, the second guy. He makes more money."

Eshwar smiled. "But in reality, the first one is wealthier. Why? Because if both of them lost their jobs today, the first guy would have a safety net, while the second would be scrambling to pay his bills. **It's not about how much you earn. It's about how much you keep.**"

Arjun leaned back, letting the words sink in. He had never thought of wealth in that way before. He had always assumed success meant making more money. But what Eshwar was saying turned that belief upside down.

Eshwar continued, "The world is full of people who drive expensive cars, live in lavish homes, and wear designer brands—but are drowning in debt. They aren't rich. They just look rich. True wealth isn't about possessions. It's about freedom."

"Freedom?" Arjun repeated.

"Yes," Eshwar said. "Financial freedom is the ability to live life on your terms, without worrying about the next paycheck. It's about having choices—whether to work or not, whether to take a break or explore new opportunities. That's what real wealth is."

Arjun exhaled slowly. He had spent years thinking that a higher salary would solve his problems. But now, he realized that without control over his expenses, no amount of money would ever be enough.

Eshwar smiled as he took a sip of tea. "Most people chase a higher income, thinking it will solve their financial worries. But income alone is not the answer. Controlling expenses, building assets, and making money work for you—that's the real game."

Arjun looked at his mentor with newfound respect.

For the first time, he saw money in a different light.

And he knew—he had to break free from the cycle of lifestyle inflation before it was too late.

The Psychological Trap

Arjun walked back home, his mind buzzing with everything Eshwar had told him.

He had never questioned his spending habits before. Every time he got a salary hike, it had felt natural to upgrade his lifestyle—better clothes, fancier restaurants, premium subscriptions, the latest phone. Wasn't that the whole point of working hard? To enjoy life's luxuries?

Yet, here he was—earning well but feeling financially trapped.

That night, as he lay in bed, he scrolled through his social media feed. His timeline was filled with pictures of colleagues and friends showcasing their latest purchases—a high-end smartwatch, an exotic vacation, a new sports bike.

Sumant had just posted a picture of himself in front of a luxury sedan with the caption: *Finally upgraded! Hard work pays off!*

A flood of likes and comments followed:

"You deserve it, bro!"

"Next stop, a sports car!"

"Living the dream!"

Arjun felt a pang of self-doubt. Was he being too cautious? Was he missing out on life by worrying about money?

The Fear of Missing Out—FOMO.

Eshwar's words from earlier echoed in his mind.

"Social pressure makes people spend beyond their means. Many people work harder, not to achieve financial freedom, but just to afford more expensive lifestyles. They aren't building wealth—they're just keeping up appearances."

For years, Arjun had unknowingly been a part of this cycle. Every festival season, he upgraded his phone, because everyone around him did. Every new restaurant that opened, he had to try it out, because his friends were doing the same. He had subscribed to multiple OTT platforms, not because he needed them all, but because cancelling them made him feel like he was missing out.

Even at work, the competition wasn't just about career growth—it extended to who wore the best brands, who dined at the trendiest places, who drove the latest model car.

The need to 'keep up' was real. And exhausting.

The worst part? He wasn't spending for himself—he was spending to impress others.

The realization stung.

He closed his eyes and tried to recall his childhood. His father had never owned a luxury car, never worn expensive brands, and never spent recklessly. Yet, he had always seemed at peace. Their family had enjoyed simple pleasures—a picnic at the park, movie nights at home, homemade sweets during festivals.

Somewhere along the way, Arjun had lost touch with that simplicity.

The world today was different. Social media constantly bombarded him with images of people living extravagant lives. And the pressure to keep up was intense.

Eshwar's words rang true: *"Lifestyle inflation is not just about money—it's about psychology. People believe they need to spend more to feel successful. But real success is about freedom, not appearances."*

For the first time in years, Arjun questioned his own choices.

Was he living life on his own terms? Or was he just chasing an illusion of success?

The Decision to Break Free

The next morning, Arjun woke up with an unusual sense of clarity. The conversation with Eshwar had planted a seed—a question that refused to be ignored.

"What if I stopped spending just to keep up? What if I took control of my money instead of letting it control me?"

For years, he had justified his spending habits with the same reasoning as Sumant—*I work hard, I deserve this.* But now, he saw things differently. What if, instead of rewarding himself with expensive things, he rewarded himself with financial security?

He picked up a notepad and wrote down two columns:

- **Needs** – The things essential for daily life.
- **Wants** – The things he could live without.

The list shocked him.

Under "Needs," he had rent, groceries, utility bills, and basic transportation.

Under "Wants," the list was much longer—premium OTT subscriptions, frequent online shopping, eating out three times a week, buying the latest gadgets, gym membership at an expensive fitness club he barely attended.

It became obvious. His financial stress wasn't because he didn't earn enough—it was because he spent without thinking.

The Challenge Begins

Arjun decided to take Eshwar's challenge seriously.

For the next month, he would:

- Track every rupee he spent.
- Differentiate between "needs" and "wants."
- Cut down unnecessary expenses and redirect that money toward savings.

The first step was cancelling subscriptions he didn't need. He downgraded to a basic mobile plan, unsubscribed from services he rarely used, and even skipped ordering food online. Instead, he and Suneetha started cooking meals together at home—a simple change that not only saved money but also brought them closer.

When friends invited him to expensive outings, he politely declined or suggested budget-friendly alternatives.

At first, it felt strange. He was so used to impulsive spending that saying *no* felt unnatural. But as the days passed, he started feeling something unexpected—*relief.*

For the first time in years, he wasn't stressed about his next paycheck. He wasn't worried about his credit card bill. He wasn't chasing a lifestyle that left him feeling empty.

Seeing the Results

At the end of the month, Arjun reviewed his expense tracker. He had saved more in those four weeks than he had in the past six months combined.

It wasn't just about the money—he felt *in control.*

Suneetha noticed the change too. "You seem different," she said one evening. "More... relaxed."

He smiled. "I finally realized that earning more isn't the key to financial success. It's about keeping more."

The shift in mindset was profound. For the first time, he wasn't dreaming about earning a higher salary—he was dreaming about *freedom.*

And this was just the beginning.

Key Takeaways from Chapter 3:
1. The Illusion of Progress

- Arjun starts tracking his expenses and realizes he is spending excessively.
- His salary increases over the years, but his savings remain negligible.
- Unnecessary spending on online shopping, dining out, and subscriptions drains his finances.

2. Sumant's Overspending Mindset

- Sumant believes money is meant to be spent, not saved.
- He upgrades his lifestyle with every salary hike—leasing luxury cars, dining at high-end restaurants, and traveling lavishly.
- Arjun begins to wonder if Sumant is truly wealthy or just maintaining an illusion of wealth.

3. Eshwar's Lesson on Lifestyle Inflation

- Eshwar explains how lifestyle inflation traps people into working harder just to afford more expensive lifestyles.
- Many believe that higher income equals financial success, but true wealth is about keeping and growing money.
- Eshwar gives a simple example:

  - A person earning ₹50,000 and saving ₹10,000 is wealthier than someone earning ₹1 lakh and saving nothing.
  - "It's not what you earn, but what you keep that matters."

4. The Psychological Trap

- Social pressure and FOMO (Fear of Missing Out) push people into spending more than they can afford.
- Instead of working to become free, most people work to maintain a high-cost lifestyle.
- Arjun realizes that even with future salary hikes, he will remain financially trapped unless he changes his mindset.

5. The Decision to Break Free

- Arjun creates a list of *Needs vs. Wants* and is shocked at how much he spends on non-essentials.
- He accepts Eshwar's challenge to track his expenses for a month.
- By cutting down unnecessary expenses, he saves more than ever before.
- The result: He feels a sense of *control* over his money for the first time.
- Arjun understands that financial freedom doesn't come from earning more, but from spending wisely and growing wealth.

CHAPTER FOUR

The first Step – Saving with Purpose

The Wake-Up Call

Arjun sat at his desk late at night, the glow of his laptop screen reflecting off his tired eyes. Numbers danced before him, statements of income and expenses, yet no matter how many times he recalculated, the conclusion remained the same—his financial situation was dire. The awareness had been slowly creeping up on him ever since his conversations with Eshwar, but now, staring at his bank statements, it was impossible to ignore.

He earned a respectable salary, yet at the end of every month, his account barely held enough to get him through the next pay cycle. It was a frustrating paradox—he worked hard, he earned well, yet he had nothing to show for it. Where did all his money go?

Determined to get to the bottom of this, Arjun pulled up his past bank statements for the last six months. As he started categorizing his expenses, the truth hit him like a punch to the gut.

Dining out at fancy restaurants, subscriptions to multiple streaming services, impulsive online shopping sprees, buying the latest gadgets just because they were trending—his lifestyle was bleeding him dry. What was even more disturbing was that he had never really thought twice about it. His mindset had always been: "I work hard; I deserve to enjoy my money." But now, he could see the reality—he wasn't enjoying his money; he was wasting it.

His mind wandered to the financial emergency he had faced just a few weeks ago when Suneetha had to be rushed to the hospital due to a sudden illness. The hospital bill had come to   ₹2 lakh, and he had been completely unprepared. He had no emergency fund, no savings to fall back on. The only way out had been to swipe his credit card, pushing himself into high-interest debt.

Even now, the credit card bill loomed over him, a reminder of his financial recklessness. He had justified his lifestyle choices with the idea that he was young and had time to save later. But when the emergency struck, his paycheck offered him no protection.

With a deep sigh, Arjun leaned back in his chair. He had been living under an illusion—a false sense of financial security just because he had a steady income. But the truth was, he was one unexpected expense away from disaster at any given moment.

For the first time, he felt a deep sense of urgency. He needed to take control of his money, or his money would always control him.

Determined, he grabbed a notepad and wrote down his first financial goal: **Start saving. No matter what.**

The Power of Paying Yourself First

Arjun couldn't shake off Eshwar's words from their last conversation. As he sat in his living room, reviewing his bank statements over the past year, a realization hit him like a tidal wave—he had been living paycheck to paycheck, despite his increasing salary. There was no structure, no discipline, just a cycle of earning and spending without purpose.

Determined to change, he met Eshwar again, eager for guidance.

"How do I even begin saving?" Arjun asked, frustration evident in his voice.

Eshwar smiled knowingly. "Most people approach saving the wrong way. They spend first and save what's left. But let me tell you a secret—wealthy people do the opposite. They pay themselves first."

"Pay myself first?" Arjun repeated, confused.

"Yes," Eshwar nodded. "The moment you receive your salary, before paying any bills, before spending a single rupee, set aside a fixed portion for yourself—your future self."

Arjun frowned. "But what if I don't have enough left for my expenses?"

"That's the trick," Eshwar said. "If you make saving your priority, your expenses will adjust automatically. Think about it—when your income increases, do you consciously decide to spend more, or does it just happen?"

Arjun thought for a moment. Every salary hike he had received led to lifestyle upgrades—a bigger house, a better car, costlier vacations. He never planned to spend more; it just happened.

Eshwar continued, "That's human nature. But what if, from today, you set aside 20% of your income the moment you receive it? You will naturally learn to manage the rest."

Arjun was skeptical but intrigued. "But isn't that difficult?"

"It's only difficult if you leave it to willpower," Eshwar said with a grin. "That's why you automate it."

Making Saving Automatic

Eshwar introduced Arjun to the concept of automatic savings. Instead of relying on self-discipline, he suggested setting up an auto-transfer so that as soon as Arjun's salary was credited, a portion would automatically move to a separate account.

"Treat it like a non-negotiable expense," Eshwar advised. "Just like you pay rent or your electricity bill, this is your 'future wealth bill.'"

Arjun immediately set up an auto-debit for a Systematic Investment Plan (SIP) in a mutual fund and a recurring deposit for emergency savings. Within minutes, he had taken his first real step toward financial stability.

For the first time in his life, he felt in control of his money, instead of money controlling him. The journey had begun.

The 50-30-20 Rule

The following evening, Arjun found himself back at the cozy cafe, notebook in hand, eager to absorb more wisdom from Eshwar. The events of the past few weeks had already ignited a shift in his thinking, and now he was ready to take concrete steps toward financial security.

Eshwar sipped his tea calmly and said, "Now that you've understood the importance of saving, the next step is knowing how to manage your income efficiently. Let me introduce you to a simple yet powerful budgeting principle—the 50-30-20 rule."

Arjun leaned in, intrigued. "50-30-20? What's that?"

Eshwar smiled. "It's a structured way to allocate your income. Fifty percent of your earnings should go toward necessities—things like rent, groceries, utilities, and essential expenses. The next thirty percent can be used for discretionary spending—entertainment, dining out, shopping, vacations, hobbies, and other personal indulgences. Finally, twenty percent should be allocated toward savings and investments. This way, you ensure financial stability without depriving yourself of life's pleasures."

Arjun took a moment to process this. He had never thought of categorizing his spending in such a manner. His expenses were more haphazard—money flowed in, and by the end of the month, it somehow disappeared. The idea of giving each rupee a designated purpose made perfect sense.

"That sounds simple," he admitted. "But I have a feeling I've been spending way too much on the 'wants' category."

Eshwar chuckled. "Most people do. It's easy to justify impulse purchases and lifestyle upgrades when you have money in hand. The problem is, without a structured approach, you never really know where your money is going."

Arjun decided to pull up his bank statements on his phone. As he skimmed through them, a realization hit him like a ton of bricks. His biggest expenses weren't always necessary ones. In just the past two months, he had spent thousands on online shopping, frequent restaurant visits, and multiple OTT platform subscriptions that he barely used.

"I knew I was overspending, but this... this is eye-opening," he muttered, shaking his head. "I spend more on eating out than I do on groceries!"

Eshwar nodded knowingly. "And that's exactly why budgeting is crucial. Most people don't intentionally mismanage their money—it happens gradually, one small expense at a time. By the time they realize it, they're stuck in a cycle of paycheck-to-paycheck living."

"So, if I strictly follow the 50-30-20 rule, I should be saving 20% every month?"

"Yes, and ideally, you should prioritize saving and investing that 20% before you even think about spending the rest. If you wait until the end of the month to save whatever is left, chances are, nothing will be left. Pay yourself first, then manage the remaining 80% wisely."

Arjun scribbled down notes furiously. He had never been this disciplined with money before, but he could see the logic behind it. "But what if my current expenses don't fit this rule? I mean, what if my rent and necessities take up more than 50%?"

Eshwar leaned back and considered the question. "That's a valid concern. The 50-30-20 rule isn't a rigid formula—it's a guideline. If your essentials consume more than 50%, you'll need to adjust. Perhaps you cut back a little on discretionary expenses, or maybe you aim to increase your income over time. The key is to maintain a balance and ensure you're consistently saving."

Arjun appreciated the flexibility of the rule. "I think I can make this work," he said, feeling determined. "I'll review my expenses and see where I can make adjustments."

Eshwar smiled. "Good. Remember, financial discipline isn't about restriction—it's about making conscious choices. If you follow this principle consistently, you'll start seeing the difference in just a few months."

Paying Off Debt Within the 50-30-20 Rule

Just as Arjun was about to close his notebook, a thought struck him. "Eshwar, what if someone has loans? Where does debt repayment fit into this rule?"

Eshwar's expression turned serious. "That's an important question. If you have outstanding debts—credit card dues, personal loans, or other liabilities—you need to prioritize paying them off. High-interest debt, like credit card balances, can erode your wealth faster than any savings or investments can grow."

Arjun nodded. "So, does that mean I should stop saving and focus entirely on repaying my debts?"

"Not entirely," Eshwar clarified. "Here's how you can approach it: If you have high-interest debt, you should use a portion of your 20% savings allocation to aggressively pay it down while still keeping a small emergency fund intact. This prevents you from falling into a worse financial trap if unexpected expenses arise."

Arjun noted this down. "So, let's say I have a credit card bill of   ₹50,000. Should I use all of my savings allocation to clear it first?"

"Ideally, yes," Eshwar affirmed. "If the interest rate is high, paying it off should be your top priority. However, if it's a low-interest loan, like a home loan, you can continue making regular payments while still saving and investing. The key is to prioritize efficiently."

"That makes sense. So, essentially, I need to categorize debt as 'urgent' or 'manageable' and plan accordingly?"

"Exactly," Eshwar said. "The goal is to get rid of bad debt—especially high-interest loans—as soon as possible. Once your debts are under control, you can allocate the full 20% to savings and investments."

Arjun felt a renewed sense of clarity. Not only did he now understand how to budget his expenses, but he also had a clear plan for tackling debt without compromising his long-term financial goals.

As he left the cafe that night, he felt lighter. The stress of managing his money was beginning to fade. With the 50-30-20 rule guiding his spending and a clear strategy for debt repayment, he was finally building the financial foundation he had always lacked.

His journey toward financial freedom had officially begun.

Sumant's Opposing View

Arjun was eager to share his newfound financial discipline with Sumant. Over a casual evening coffee at their favorite café, he laid out everything he had learned from Eshwar—the importance of saving, the power of investing, and how he was now automatically setting aside 20% of his income. Expecting admiration or even curiosity, Arjun was taken aback by Sumant's reaction.

Sumant chuckled, shaking his head as he stirred his cappuccino. "You're overthinking all this, Arjun. Life is meant to be enjoyed! What's the point of working so hard if you're just going to lock away your money? Live a little!"

Arjun frowned, setting his cup down. "But what if there's an emergency? What if we lose our jobs? Shouldn't we have something to fall back on?"

Sumant leaned back, waving his hand dismissively. "We'll figure it out when the time comes. Anyway, I have my salary, my credit cards, and a good credit score. If I ever need money, I can always take a personal loan. That's what banks are for!"

Arjun sighed. He knew this mindset all too well—because it was his own just a few weeks ago. He had been living paycheck to paycheck, assuming that as long as his salary arrived on time, everything would be fine. But then he had met Eshwar, and the conversation had changed his perspective forever. Financial security wasn't about earning more; it was about keeping more.

"I used to think like that too," Arjun admitted. "But then I realized that no matter how much I earned, I never felt secure. That's not freedom, Sumant. That's a trap."

Sumant laughed, shaking his head. "You sound like an old man! We're young, we should enjoy our lives. What's the point of money if you don't spend it on experiences? I work hard—I deserve to reward myself."

Arjun could see that Sumant was genuinely convinced of his lifestyle. He had always been the kind of person who lived in the moment, indulging in weekend getaways, expensive restaurants, and the latest gadgets. He believed that money should be spent while one was young enough to enjoy it.

"I'm not saying don't enjoy life," Arjun replied. "But imagine this—you're on a ship in the middle of the ocean. Right now, the sea is calm, and you're having a great time. But what if a storm hits? Wouldn't you rather have a life jacket ready instead of trying to build one when the waves are already crashing?"

Sumant scoffed. "A bit dramatic, don't you think? Look, I get what you're saying, but you can't live in fear. If something happens, we'll deal with it then. Right now, I'd rather enjoy my life than stress about the future."

Arjun exhaled deeply. "I understand. I used to think saving was a sacrifice, but it's actually the opposite. It gives you choices. Imagine if you saved just 20% of your income for the next five years. You'd have a solid emergency fund, maybe even enough to start investing seriously. Then, when you want to take a vacation, you can do it without guilt or debt. Doesn't that sound better than relying on credit cards?"

Sumant shrugged. "Debt isn't always a bad thing. My bank offers me loans at low interest rates. As long as I can pay the EMIs, what's the harm?"

Arjun shook his head. "That's the problem. You're assuming your income will always cover your expenses. But what if something unexpected happens—job loss, a medical emergency? The people who struggle the most during tough times are those who never planned for them."

Sumant paused for a moment, as if considering Arjun's words, but then shook his head again. "I just don't see the point of restricting myself now for a future that's uncertain. What if I die tomorrow? What good would my savings do then?"

Arjun gave a small smile. "What if you live till 90? What will you do then? Keep working forever? Borrowing money to survive?"

Sumant rolled his eyes. "I'll cross that bridge when I get there. For now, I'd rather enjoy my life."

Arjun realized that Sumant's mindset wasn't unique. Many people believed that financial planning was for later in life. But he no longer wanted to leave his future to chance. He had already felt the pain of financial stress, and he wasn't willing to go back.

Instead of arguing further, he decided to let his actions speak. Over time, he knew that his financial discipline would lead to a future where he didn't have to worry about money—while people like Sumant would remain trapped in the endless cycle of earning and spending.

As the two friends parted ways that evening, Arjun couldn't help but feel a quiet sense of determination. He had chosen his path, and he knew it would make all the difference in the long run.

The First Victory

As the first month of his new financial discipline came to an end, Arjun logged into his bank account with a mix of curiosity and anticipation. A sense of satisfaction spread across his face as he saw the numbers on the screen—his savings account had grown for the first time in years. It wasn't a massive sum, but it was real. More importantly, it was his.

For the past month, he had followed Eshwar's advice diligently. The automatic transfer of 20% from his salary had happened seamlessly, without him even having to think about it. At the beginning of the month, he had worried that saving would make his life miserable—that he'd feel restricted, deprived of his usual comforts. But to his surprise, that hadn't been the case at all.

He had still gone out for coffee, still enjoyed dinner with Suneetha, still met friends on the weekends. The only difference was that he had been mindful. Instead of impulsively ordering food every evening, he and Suneetha had rediscovered the joy of cooking together. Instead of aimlessly browsing online stores and buying things he didn't really need, he had learned to pause and ask himself, *Do I really need this?* More often than not, the answer was no.

More Money, Same Happiness

As he compared his expenses from previous months, something struck him—he didn't feel any less happy than before. In fact, he felt better. There was a quiet satisfaction in knowing that his money wasn't just disappearing as soon as it came in. It was working for him.

At work, he no longer felt the usual anxiety at the end of the month, wondering how he'd make it till the next paycheck. He no longer dreaded unexpected expenses. For the first time in his life, he had a buffer.

One evening, as he and Suneetha sat on their balcony enjoying tea, he shared his feelings with her.

"You know, I thought this whole 'saving money' thing would make me feel restricted. But honestly, I feel... free."

Suneetha smiled. "That's because you're finally in control. Earlier, money controlled you. Now, you control it."

Her words hit him hard. That was exactly it. He had spent years chasing money, spending it as soon as he earned it, always feeling like he never had enough. But now, with a simple change in habit, everything felt different.

Confidence in the Future

A week later, he met Eshwar for their usual discussion at the park.

"So, how does it feel to be a saver?" Eshwar asked with a knowing smile.

Arjun laughed. "Strange, actually. I used to think people who saved a lot were missing out on life. But now I see it's the opposite. I don't feel deprived—I feel secure."

"That's your first victory," Eshwar said. "The moment you realize that saving isn't about sacrifice, but about gaining control over your life."

Arjun nodded. "For the first time, I'm actually looking forward to my financial future."

Eshwar placed a hand on his shoulder. "This is just the beginning, Arjun. Now that you have the foundation, it's time to build something bigger."

Arjun knew exactly what Eshwar meant. He had won his first battle, but the war for true financial freedom was just beginning.

*****

Here are the important points to be noted from "**The First Victory**":

1. Arjun's First Savings Experience

- At the end of the month, Arjun sees his savings grow for the first time.
- He realizes that saving money doesn't feel like a burden but a source of satisfaction.
- The automatic transfer of 20% of his salary happened without effort, making saving easy.

2. No Feeling of Deprivation

- Arjun was initially worried that cutting expenses would make him feel restricted.
- However, he continues enjoying life—going for coffee, eating out occasionally, and spending time with friends.
- Small changes, like cooking at home instead of ordering food, help him save without reducing his happiness.

3. Money Is No Longer Controlling Him

- Arjun notices a shift in his mindset—he now questions unnecessary purchases before spending.
- Unlike before, he no longer feels anxious at the end of the month.
- Having a financial buffer gives him peace of mind and confidence.

4. Discussion with Suneetha

- Arjun shares his newfound sense of freedom with Suneetha.

- She points out that earlier, money controlled him, but now he controls money.
- This realization strengthens his commitment to financial discipline.

5. Meeting with Eshwar – A New Perspective on Savings

- Arjun meets Eshwar and admits that saving doesn't feel restrictive but empowering.
- Eshwar calls this his "first victory"—understanding that saving isn't about sacrifice but control.
- Arjun now looks forward to his financial future, realizing this is just the beginning of his financial journey.

CHAPTER FIVE

Escaping the Debt Trap

1. The Illusion of Easy Money

Arjun sat in his study, a cup of tea slowly cooling beside him as he sifted through old bank statements, credit card bills, and loan documents. He hadn't paid much attention to them in the past—only glancing at the minimum due and making sure he had enough in his account to cover it. But today was different. Today, he wanted to confront the truth.

As he flipped through the pages, the numbers painted a painful story.

Swipe. ₹4,500. Dinner at a five-star hotel.

Swipe. ₹12,000. A weekend getaway.

Swipe. ₹1,35,000. The latest smartphone and accessories.

EMI deducted: ₹21,000. Car loan.

EMI deducted: ₹40,000. Home loan.

EMI deducted: ₹8,500. Personal loan.

Late fee: ₹950. Credit card.

Arjun let out a slow breath. It was all there in black and white. The life he had built—his fancy car, the international vacations, the premium lifestyle—hadn't been funded by his success. It had been funded by debt.

The First Swipe—The Beginning of the Trap

It all started when he got his first job. The HR department had handed him a welcome kit on his joining day, which included a neatly packed envelope from a bank. Inside was his salary account details and an *exclusive* pre-approved credit card offer.

"Congratulations, Mr. Arjun! You are eligible for a ₹2 lakh credit limit. No documents required!"

He had felt a strange sense of accomplishment at that moment. A credit card. It was a symbol of financial independence, wasn't it? The world saw people with credit cards as responsible, successful individuals. He had signed up without hesitation.

The first few months, he had used it sparingly—mostly for online purchases and occasional dining. The bank's mobile app made things easy, showing only the **minimum amount due** each month. Just ₹2,000 or ₹3,000? That seemed manageable.

Then came the next tempting offer.

"Congratulations! Your credit limit has been increased to ₹3.5 lakh."

He had felt wealthier than ever. If banks were increasing his credit limit, it must mean he was doing well, right?

The Lifestyle Inflation—Living Beyond Means

Arjun's spending started to increase. He had once been comfortable with a ₹500 meal at a regular restaurant, but now, fine-dining at ₹3,000 per meal seemed justified.

"What's the point of working hard if you can't enjoy life?" he would tell himself.

His social circle changed, too. Most of his friends had credit cards and loans, and they often compared their possessions.

"I just got the latest iPhone on EMI—only ₹4,500 per month!"
"Planning a trip to Bali next month! I booked everything on my credit card."

Everyone was doing it. Why should he hold back?

Then came the loans.

- A **personal loan** to cover a vacation to the Maldives. *Because why wait when I can experience it now?*
- A **car loan** because his colleagues had upgraded their vehicles, and he didn't want to be the odd one out. *A bigger car makes a better impression.*
- A **home loan**—his biggest financial commitment. The bank had convinced him, *You deserve a bigger house! Property prices always go up!*

Each decision had seemed *rational* at the time. The banks and financial advisors always had persuasive arguments.

"You're not spending, you're investing in your lifestyle."
"EMIs are just a fraction of your salary. You won't even feel the pinch."
"This is how smart people manage money."

But now, years later, Arjun was looking at his bank statements and realizing that these small, *manageable* EMIs had snowballed into a financial straitjacket.

The Illusion of Financial Success

For years, Arjun had mistaken *access to money* for *having money.*

Having a ₹10 lakh credit limit did not mean he had ₹10 lakh.

Being eligible for a ₹50 lakh loan did not mean he had ₹50 lakh in wealth.

It was a dangerous illusion.

Whenever he bought something, he had felt a momentary high—the excitement of owning the latest gadget, the thrill of booking an exotic vacation. But those feelings faded quickly, replaced by the burden of paying off the debt.

The *real* high had been when he saw his salary credited at the beginning of the month. But within a few days, most of it was gone—swallowed by loan payments, credit card dues, and interest charges.

He wasn't *earning* for himself. He was earning for the banks.

The Breaking Point—A Moment of Realization

The wake-up call came when he tried to calculate how much of his salary was actually his to spend freely.

His monthly salary: ₹1,50,000

Total EMIs and credit card payments: ₹98,500

Remaining for daily expenses, savings, and investments: ₹51,500

Less than 35% of his income was actually his. The rest belonged to the banks.

And if he lost his job? He wouldn't last more than two months.

That thought hit him like a thunderbolt.

"What have I done?"

He was trapped in a cycle of earning and repaying. He was not financially free. He was *financially enslaved*.

That night, as he looked around his apartment—filled with expensive furniture, high-end electronics, and designer clothes—he saw them differently. These were not *his* possessions. They were things he had borrowed from the future.

It was time to change.

It was time to escape the debt trap.

2. The Reality Check

It was a quiet evening at Eshwar's home. The aroma of freshly brewed coffee filled the air as Arjun sat across from his mentor. The usual confidence in his voice was missing. Instead, there was hesitation, uncertainty.

Eshwar noticed it immediately. He had seen this look before—the look of someone burdened by financial stress but unsure how to escape it.

"Something on your mind, Arjun?" Eshwar asked, taking a slow sip of his coffee.

Arjun hesitated for a moment, then exhaled deeply.

"Eshwar, I feel stuck. I make decent money, yet I never seem to have enough. Every month, my salary comes in, and within days, it vanishes. I don't even know where it goes."

Eshwar leaned back, listening intently.

"I have a house, a car, a good lifestyle—but I feel like I'm running on a treadmill. No matter how hard I work, I'm not moving forward financially."

Eshwar nodded knowingly. "Let's do a simple exercise. Tell me—how much of your income goes toward loan payments?"

Arjun frowned. "I'm not sure. I just pay the EMIs as they come."

"Then let's calculate it now."

Eshwar handed him a notepad and pen. "List down all your monthly loan payments—everything, including your credit cards."

Arjun scribbled down the numbers one by one.

Loan Type	EMI Amount (₹)
Home Loan	40,000
Car Loan	21,000
Personal Loan	8,500
Credit Card Minimum Payment	12,000
Consumer Durable Loans (Appliances, Gadgets, etc.)	4,000
Total Monthly Loan Payments	**₹85,500**

Arjun stared at the total. His heart sank.

"   **₹85,500...**" He whispered, as if saying it out loud would make it real.

"And what's your monthly salary?"

"   **₹1,50,000.**"

Eshwar nodded. "So before you even think about groceries, utility bills, fuel, entertainment, savings, or investments, more than half of your salary is already gone."

Arjun gulped. He had never thought about it this way.

Eshwar continued, "Now, let's add your monthly expenses—just an estimate."

Expense Type	Amount (₹)
Rent & Maintenance	15,000
Groceries & Essentials	12,000
Utility Bills (Electricity, Water, Internet, etc.)	7,500
Fuel & Transportation	6,000
Dining & Entertainment	10,000
Miscellaneous	5,000
Total Expenses	**₹55,500**

Arjun's mind raced.

Total EMIs + Expenses: ₹85,500 + ₹55,500 = ₹1,41,000

Salary Left After Everything: ₹9,000

He leaned back in shock. "Is this all I have left at the end of the month?"

Eshwar let the silence linger, allowing Arjun to absorb the weight of reality.

"And what if there's an emergency?" Eshwar asked.

Arjun's throat felt dry. He knew the answer.

"I take another loan... or swipe my credit card."

Eshwar sighed. "That's how debt traps work, Arjun. The more you rely on loans, the more you become dependent on them. Your future salary is already spent before you even earn it."

Arjun rubbed his temples. "I never looked at my finances like this before. I thought I was doing well because I could afford the EMIs. But I'm not building wealth—I'm just paying banks every month."

Eshwar smiled gently. **"Debt is a silent thief, Arjun. It steals your future income. Every EMI you pay is money you're taking away from your future self."**

Arjun looked at the notepad again. The numbers didn't lie. He had worked hard for years, but he had never truly owned his income.

It was time to change that.

He needed a plan. He needed a way out of this financial mess.

3. Understanding Good Debt vs. Bad Debt

The weight of his financial reality still pressed heavily on Arjun's shoulders. He had never imagined that more than half of his salary was disappearing into EMIs. He thought he was managing well, but now, he realized—he was merely surviving.

Eshwar sensed Arjun's turmoil and decided it was time to introduce a crucial concept. He placed his coffee mug down and leaned forward.

"Arjun, let me ask you something—do you think all debt is bad?"

Arjun nodded without hesitation. "Of course! Debt is ruining my life, isn't it?"

Eshwar chuckled. "Not necessarily. There's a difference between good debt and bad debt. The problem isn't debt itself—it's the kind of debt you take on and how you manage it."

Arjun frowned. "Good debt? That sounds contradictory."

Eshwar pulled out a piece of paper and drew two columns. At the top, he wrote:

? **Good Debt** vs. **Bad Debt**

Good Debt

Home Loan*(if within your means)*

- A house is an appreciating asset if bought wisely.
- Instead of paying rent, you build equity in a property over time.
- Interest rates on home loans are lower compared to personal loans or credit cards.
- Tax benefits reduce the overall cost of borrowing.

Business Loan*(if it generates income)*

- If borrowed for the right reasons, it can grow your wealth.
- The key is ensuring the business can generate more returns than the interest paid.

Education Loan*(if it improves earning potential)*

- Investing in the right education can lead to higher salaries and career growth.
- The loan should be taken only when necessary and for quality education with a clear career path.

Bad Debt

Credit Card Debt

- One of the highest interest rates (30-40% annually).
- Encourages reckless spending because of the illusion of "easy money."

- Minimum payments trap you in an endless cycle of debt.

Personal Loans*(for non-essential expenses)*

- Often taken for vacations, weddings, or gadgets.
- No asset or investment is created, only debt.

Car Loans

- A car is a depreciating asset—it loses value the moment you drive it off the showroom floor.
- Paying EMIs for something that loses value doesn't make financial sense unless absolutely necessary.

Consumer Durable Loans*(for lifestyle upgrades)*

- Buying the latest phone, TV, or gadgets on EMI is a bad financial habit.
- These items lose value quickly, yet the loan stays with you for years.

Arjun stared at the list. It was eye-opening. He had always thought of loans as a way to afford things, but he had never questioned **why** he was taking them.

"So, my home loan is not a bad thing?" he asked.

Eshwar smiled. "Not if it's within your means. A home can be an appreciating asset, but only if you're not overburdened with EMIs. The key is balance."

"But my car loan—that's bad debt?" Arjun asked, his voice laced with regret.

Eshwar nodded. "It depends. If your job absolutely requires a car, it's a necessary expense. But if you could have bought a more affordable model or managed without one, then yes—it's bad debt."

Arjun felt a sinking feeling in his stomach. **"Most of my debt is bad debt."**

Eshwar patted his shoulder. "That's okay. The important thing is that you now understand the difference. You've already taken the first step—awareness."

Arjun nodded, determination replacing the regret. **"Now, I need to fix it."**

Eshwar smiled. "Exactly. And I'll show you how. There are two proven methods to clear debt strategically—the Snowball and Avalanche methods. Let's dive into those next."

4. The Debt Snowball vs. Avalanche Methods

Arjun now understood the weight of his financial choices. His mind buzzed with questions—How do I fix this mess? Should I pay off my loans randomly? Should I focus on the biggest one first? Or the smallest one?

Eshwar could see the storm of thoughts raging inside Arjun. He leaned back, took a sip of his tea, and said, **"There's a strategic way to clear your debts. In fact, there are two popular methods—Debt Snowball and Debt Avalanche."**

Arjun leaned forward, intrigued. **"Two methods? What's the difference?"**

Eshwar grabbed a notepad and started drawing:

Debt Snowball Method (Psychological Boost)

1. List all your debts from smallest to largest, regardless of interest rates.
2. Pay the minimum amount on all debts except the smallest one.
3. Channel all extra money into repaying the smallest debt first.

4. Once the smallest debt is cleared, use that freed-up money to tackle the next smallest debt.
5. Repeat until all debts are gone.

Example:

- **₹15,000 Credit Card Debt** (Interest 36%)
- **₹50,000 Personal Loan** (Interest 20%)
- **₹2,00,000 Car Loan** (Interest 12%)

You start by clearing the ₹15,000 credit card debt first. Once that is gone, you take the amount you were paying toward it and attack the ₹50,000 personal loan. This continues until you're debt-free.

Why It Works?

- Provides **quick wins**, boosting motivation.
- Helps people stay committed because they **see progress faster.**

Debt Avalanche Method (Mathematical Savings)

1. List all debts from highest to lowest interest rate.
2. Pay the minimum amount on all debts except the one with the highest interest rate.
3. Channel all extra money into repaying the highest-interest debt first.
4. Once that is cleared, focus on the next highest-interest debt.
5. Repeat until debt-free.

Example:

Using the same loans above, you would start by paying off the **credit card debt first** because it has the highest **interest rate (36%)**. Then, you tackle the **personal loan (20%)**, and finally, the **car loan (12%)**.

Why It Works?

- Saves the most **money in interest payments.**
- Clears high-cost debts **faster**, making future payments more affordable.

Arjun studied both methods carefully. "The Snowball method gives psychological motivation, while the Avalanche method saves more money in the long run?"

Eshwar nodded. "Exactly. Which one do you think suits you?"

Arjun rubbed his chin. "I think the Avalanche method makes more sense for me. My credit card interest is ridiculously high. If I don't get rid of it fast, it will keep eating into my finances."

Eshwar smiled. "Good choice. Since your biggest enemy is high-interest debt, tackling that first will bring the fastest financial relief."

Arjun felt a surge of determination. "Okay. I'm ready. What's the next step?"

Eshwar's eyes gleamed. **"Now, we create a proper debt repayment plan."**

5. Creating a Debt Repayment Plan

Arjun had made his choice. **The Debt Avalanche Method.** He was now determined to eliminate his debts in the most efficient way possible. But determination alone wasn't enough—he needed a plan.

Eshwar leaned forward. "Now that you've chosen your strategy, the first step is clarity. You need to know exactly how much you owe, to whom, and at what interest rate."

Arjun nodded. **"I think I have a rough idea..."**

Eshwar raised an eyebrow. **"Rough ideas don't work in finance. Let's get precise."**

Step 1: Listing All Debts

Arjun pulled out his laptop and started listing his debts:

Loan Type	Amount Outstanding	Interest Rate (%)	Monthly EMI (₹)
Credit Card Debt	₹1,50,000	36%	₹7,500
Personal Loan	₹2,00,000	20%	₹9,500
Car Loan	₹3,50,000	12%	₹15,000
Home Loan	₹25,00,000	8%	₹30,000

When he saw the numbers clearly written down, his stomach churned. "This... this is worse than I imagined."

Eshwar simply nodded. "Most people avoid facing reality. But now that you know, you can take control."

Step 2: Identifying the Priority Debt

Eshwar pointed at the credit card debt. "This is where you begin. With a 36% interest rate, this is the deadliest of them all. Your first target is to wipe this out as fast as possible."

Arjun gulped. "But I'm already paying ₹7,500 per month toward it."

Eshwar smiled. "And how much of that actually reduces the debt?"

Arjun checked his statement. His face paled. "Only ₹2,000. The rest is just interest!"

Eshwar nodded. "Exactly. That's how credit cards trap people. Unless you aggressively attack the principal amount, you'll be paying forever."

Step 3: Budgeting for Extra Payments

Arjun needed to find extra money to accelerate his payments.

- He reviewed his expenses and **cut down discretionary spending** (dining out, subscriptions, impulse shopping).
- He decided to **temporarily pause investments** (except his emergency fund) until the high-interest debt was cleared.
- He looked for **ways to increase income**—freelance projects, weekend tutoring, selling unused items.
- He spoke to his HR about **salary restructuring** to optimize tax savings.

After calculating, he found he could **free up ₹15,000 extra every month.**

Eshwar smiled. "That's the power of awareness. Now, instead of just ₹7,500, you'll be paying ₹22,500 toward your credit card debt."

Arjun's eyes widened. "That means I can clear it in just seven months instead of years!"

Step 4: Negotiating Better Terms

Eshwar then gave him another tip. "Call your bank. Ask them if they can lower the interest rate or convert the debt into a lower-interest personal loan."

Arjun hesitated. **"Will they agree?"**

Eshwar smirked. "You'll be surprised. Banks would rather get some interest than risk you defaulting."

After a call, the bank **offered to reduce his interest rate to 24%** if he paid a lump sum immediately. Arjun used part of his emergency fund to do it—**saving himself thousands in interest.**

Step 5: Creating a Timeline

With all adjustments, Arjun created his **debt freedom roadmap**:

Month 1-7: Pay off the credit card debt completely.

Month 8-18: Focus on the personal loan next.

Month 19 onward: Attack the car loan while continuing home loan payments.

For the first time, he felt **in control.**

Arjun looked at Eshwar. "This is incredible. I never thought I could fix this mess so fast."

Eshwar smiled. **"That's the power of a plan."**

6. Sumant's Financial Crisis

While Arjun was making steady progress in escaping his debt trap, his friend Sumant was walking straight into one.

Sumant had always been a firm believer in "living life to the fullest." He often joked, "Why should I wait to enjoy life when I can buy everything on EMI?" Unlike Arjun, who had started re-evaluating his financial decisions, Sumant saw no reason to slow down.

His lifestyle was aspirational—at least on the surface. He upgraded his car to a luxury sedan, justifying it as a "status symbol" that matched his professional growth. His credit card bills swelled as he frequently dined at five-star restaurants, bought the latest gadgets, and even took international vacations—all on borrowed money. He had three credit cards, each nearing their limit, and personal loans taken out to cover previous expenses.

Despite all this, Sumant was never worried. He had a stable corporate job, a good salary, and as long as he could make his EMI payments, he saw no problem. In fact, he took pride in his financial juggling act, often teasing Arjun about his newfound "frugality."

"You only live once, my friend! What's the point of working so hard if you don't enjoy the fruits of your labour?" Sumant would say, tapping his brand-new smartwatch.

Arjun, who had started viewing money differently, tried to warn him. "Sumant, I've been in your shoes. It feels fine now, but debt can spiral out of control. What if something unexpected happens?"

Sumant laughed. "Unexpected? Like what? I have a great job. My salary covers all my EMIs. Banks wouldn't offer me credit if I couldn't afford it, right?"

Arjun sighed. He knew it was pointless to argue with someone who hadn't yet faced reality.

The Unexpected Blow

Then, one evening, Sumant's world turned upside down.

His company held an emergency meeting. Due to economic downturns and reduced profitability, management had decided to downsize. Names were read out, and before he could process what was happening, Sumant's was on the list.

Laid off.

The news hit him like a truck. He had never imagined being without a job. His identity was built around his corporate success. His first reaction was denial—this couldn't be happening. He had worked hard, delivered results. Why him?

But denial quickly turned to panic as reality set in. Without his salary, how would he pay his EMIs? His credit card bills were due next week. His car loan had another three years of payments. His house rent, personal loan, and lifestyle expenses were all dependent on his monthly paycheck.

For the first time, he opened his banking app with fear instead of excitement. His savings? Barely enough to last a month. His debts? Staggering. His entire financial world had been built on the assumption that his income would always be there. Now, without it, everything was crumbling.

Sumant frantically called a few colleagues, hoping to find another job quickly. But the market was tough, and job offers weren't coming as easily as he had hoped. The panic worsened.

Within weeks, the stress became unbearable. Collection calls from banks started coming in. His credit card company warned of late fees. His landlord reminded him that rent was due. Every financial commitment he had made was now suffocating him.

One evening, as he sat in his dimly lit apartment, staring at his growing pile of overdue bills, he thought about Arjun's warnings. Had he been right all along? Was he the fool for ignoring the risks of debt?

For the first time in his life, Sumant felt completely helpless. His high-flying lifestyle had come crashing down, and he had no backup plan.

With no one else to turn to, he picked up his phone and dialed Arjun's number.

"I need help," he admitted, his voice trembling.

And for the first time in years, he truly meant it.

8. Sumant Seeks Help

Sumant sat in his car, gripping the steering wheel tightly. The same car he had proudly driven off the showroom floor just months ago, feeling like a king. Now, it felt like a burden—another expense he couldn't afford.

His hands were sweaty as he scrolled through his phone, hesitating before pressing the call button. The last time he had spoken to Arjun, he had laughed at his frugal ways. Now, here he was, reaching out in desperation.

The phone rang twice before Arjun picked up.

"Hey, Sumant! It's been a while. How's everything?" Arjun's voice was warm, unaware of the storm brewing in his friend's life.

Sumant swallowed hard. "Arjun... I messed up," he admitted, his voice cracking. "I lost my job. My debts... they're drowning me. I don't know what to do."

There was a pause. Then, in a calm voice, Arjun said, "Where are you? Let's meet."

A Conversation That Changed Everything

An hour later, they sat in a quiet café. Sumant looked exhausted, his confident demeanour shattered. His eyes darted around nervously, as if expecting creditors to walk in any second.

Arjun listened patiently as Sumant poured out his troubles—the mounting EMIs, the maxed-out credit cards, the sleepless nights, the fear of losing everything.

When Sumant finally stopped, expecting pity or maybe a financial bailout, Arjun simply leaned forward and asked, "What do you want to do now?"

Sumant blinked. "I... I don't know. I just need money to clear these debts. I was hoping you could—"

Arjun raised a hand. "I won't lend you money."

Sumant's face fell. "But I—"

"I won't lend you money," Arjun repeated, "because that's not what you need. You don't need a quick fix, Sumant. You need a plan. You need to change your approach to money, or this will happen again."

Sumant exhaled, his shoulders slumping. "So what do I do?"

Arjun took out his notepad and started writing. "Let's start by understanding where you stand financially."

Together, they listed all of Sumant's debts—credit cards, loans, pending bills. The final amount was staggering.

"No wonder you feel suffocated," Arjun said. "But you're not beyond saving. The first step is to stop making it worse."

Sumant frowned. "What do you mean?"

"Cut all unnecessary expenses. Right now. No more shopping, no dining out, no impulsive purchases. Every rupee you spend should have a purpose—either survival or debt repayment."

Sumant nodded slowly. It felt like a drastic shift from his usual lifestyle, but he had no choice.

Learning the Principles of Financial Discipline

Over the next hour, Arjun walked him through everything he had learned from Eshwar:

- The **difference between good debt and bad debt.** Sumant had taken loans for lifestyle upgrades, not investments—this was a critical mistake.
- The **Debt Avalanche method**—paying off high-interest debts first to stop the financial bleeding.
- The importance of **having an emergency fund**—something Sumant had never considered.

- The **power of financial discipline.** Sumant realized he had never actually controlled his money—it had controlled him.

By the end of their conversation, Sumant looked drained, but there was something new in his eyes—determination.

"I don't want to live like this anymore," he said firmly. "I need to fix this."

Arjun nodded. "You can. But it won't happen overnight. You need to change your mindset first."

Sumant ran a hand through his hair. "Where do I even start?"

Arjun smiled. "With the first step—accepting that this is a long journey. Let's set up a plan."

The First Step Towards Redemption

Sumant left the café with more than just advice—he left with a strategy. He called his bank to negotiate lower interest rates. He listed out things he could sell—old gadgets, expensive but unnecessary furniture. He started looking for freelance work to generate quick income.

Most importantly, he accepted that his spending habits had to change. The latest phone model could wait. His pride could take a backseat.

For the first time in years, Sumant was thinking about money not as a tool for instant gratification, but as a responsibility.

And as he walked home that evening, he realized something—this crisis, though painful, might just be the best lesson he had ever learned.

9. Arjun's Debt-Free Milestone

The night Arjun made his final credit card payment, he sat in front of his laptop, staring at the confirmation message on the screen.

"Transaction Successful. Outstanding Balance: ₹ 0.00."

For a moment, he didn't move. He read the message again, half-expecting an error, a hidden charge, something he had overlooked. But no—his most suffocating financial burden was finally gone.

A slow smile spread across his face. The weight he had carried for years, the constant stress of high-interest debt, was gone. He closed his laptop and leaned back, exhaling deeply.

That night, for the first time in years, he slept without worrying about pending EMIs.

Experiencing the Freedom of a Debt-Free Life

The next morning, as Arjun walked to his office, something felt different. The city was the same—the honking cars, the rush-hour chaos, the billboards advertising things he no longer craved. But he felt lighter, as if an invisible chain had been broken.

He wasn't worried about the next billing cycle. He wasn't dreading late fees. He wasn't calculating minimum payments in his head.

He was free.

During his lunch break, he checked his bank balance out of habit. But this time, instead of mentally allocating funds to debt payments, he had a different question in mind:

"Where should I invest this money?"

Redirecting His Money Toward Growth

Eshwar had always told him, "Every rupee you earn should either work for you or protect you." Now that his salary wasn't vanishing into credit card bills, Arjun was ready to follow that principle.

He had two clear priorities:

1. **Building an emergency fund** – He wanted at least six months' worth of living expenses set aside in a liquid account. This would ensure that no unexpected event would push him back into debt.
2. **Investing for the future** – Instead of letting his money sit idle, he planned to invest systematically in mutual funds and stocks, allowing it to grow over time.

That evening, he called Eshwar. "I did it," he said simply.

Eshwar chuckled. "Feels good, doesn't it?"

"More than I expected," Arjun admitted. "I always thought being debt-free just meant avoiding stress. But it's more than that. It's... liberating."

"Because you're in control now," Eshwar said. "Debt makes people slaves to money. Now, you're making money work for you."

Arjun nodded. He had seen the consequences of bad financial decisions through Sumant's struggles. But now, he had also experienced the rewards of financial discipline firsthand.

A New Perspective on Money

A week later, Arjun walked past a mall where he once impulsively bought things on credit. He saw a new smartphone ad, the kind that would have tempted him in the past.

This time, he smiled and kept walking.

He didn't need to impress anyone. He didn't need instant gratification. He was working toward something bigger—financial independence.

And for the first time in his life, he knew he was on the right path.

*****

Key Takeaways from This Chapter

✓ **Debt steals your future income** – The more loans you take, the more of your salary is locked away in EMIs, limiting your financial freedom.

✓ **Understand the difference between good debt and bad debt** – Loans for income-generating assets (like a home within your means or an investment in education) can be beneficial. However, high-interest debts like credit cards, personal loans, and car loans often lead to financial stress.

✓ **Control your credit usage** – Credit cards are not free money. If not managed wisely, they can become a financial trap with high-interest burdens.

✓ **Choose a debt repayment strategy that works for you** – The **Debt Avalanche Method** (paying off high-interest debt first) minimizes total interest paid, while the **Debt Snowball Method** (starting with the smallest debt for psychological wins) builds momentum.

✓ **Avoid lifestyle inflation** – Increasing your expenses just because you earn more will keep you trapped in a cycle of debt.

✓ **Build an emergency fund** – Having 6–12 months' worth of living expenses set aside protects you from unexpected financial crises.

✓ **Invest the money you free up** – Once debts are cleared, redirect the money toward wealth-building investments instead of unnecessary spending.

✓ **True financial freedom comes from control over money** – Becoming debt-free isn't just about avoiding stress; it's about taking charge of your finances and securing your future.

CHAPTER SIX

Building an Emergency Fund

The Unexpected Storm

Arjun had never felt this kind of financial confidence before. Ever since he cleared his credit card debt, a new sense of control over his money had emerged. He no longer worried about unpaid dues or accumulating interest. Every rupee in his account now had a purpose, and that purpose was his financial security.

One evening, as he was wrapping up work, his phone rang. It was his father, and his voice sounded tense.

"Arjun, your mother isn't feeling well. She suddenly collapsed, and we had to rush her to the hospital. The doctors are running tests, but they need an immediate deposit for further treatment. Can you arrange the money?"

A year ago, such a call would have sent Arjun into a panic. He would have scrambled to check his credit limit, debated taking a personal loan, or considered borrowing money from friends. But today, he was prepared.

"Don't worry, Dad. I'll transfer the money right away," he said calmly.

Opening his banking app, he swiftly transferred the required amount from his emergency fund. There was no anxiety, no last-minute struggle—just a smooth transaction that ensured his mother got the medical attention she needed. As he rushed to the hospital, a thought crossed his mind: *This is why I built an emergency fund.*

Later that night, sitting beside his recovering mother, he reflected on how different things would have been if he had not planned ahead. This was the moment he truly understood that financial security wasn't just about numbers—it was about peace of mind.

2. Eshwar's Lesson: Life is Unpredictable

A few days later, over a cup of tea at their usual café, Arjun shared the experience with Eshwar.

"Thankfully, I had my emergency fund, Eshwar. Otherwise, I don't know what I would have done."

Eshwar smiled knowingly. "Most people assume they can handle emergencies when they arise. But in reality, when the storm hits, they scramble for money. And that's when they make the worst financial mistakes."

Arjun nodded, remembering his own past habits. "Like swiping a credit card without thinking about the consequences," he said.

"Exactly," Eshwar continued. "When people don't have emergency savings, they resort to quick-fix solutions that create long-term problems." He listed out the common mistakes people make:

- Swiping credit cards and accumulating high-interest debt.
- Taking personal loans with unreasonable repayment terms.
- Selling long-term investments at a loss to cover short-term needs.

- Borrowing money from friends and family, which can strain relationships.

"An emergency fund is not just about money—it's about avoiding desperation. When you have one, you make decisions from a place of strength, not fear."

Hearing this, Arjun felt a deep sense of gratitude. He had experienced firsthand how financial planning had transformed his response to an unexpected crisis. And he was determined never to go back to his old ways.

3. Understanding the Emergency Fund

After finishing his tea, Arjun leans forward, eager to learn more. "So, Eshwar, how exactly does an emergency fund work?" he asks.

Eshwar smiles, appreciating Arjun's growing curiosity. "An emergency fund is not about earning high returns," he begins. "It's about financial security. It's a safety net that keeps you from making bad financial decisions in desperate situations."

Arjun nods, recalling the past instances when he had borrowed money to cover unexpected expenses. "So, it's like a financial shock absorber?" he asks.

"Exactly," Eshwar agrees. "It's a reserve of money set aside exclusively for sudden, unavoidable expenses—like medical emergencies, urgent home repairs, or even job loss. It ensures that you don't have to rely on high-interest loans or liquidate long-term investments during tough times."

How Much Should You Save?

Arjun frowns, thinking about how much he should put aside. "But how much is enough?"

"That depends on your financial commitments," Eshwar explains. "A single person might get by with six months' worth of expenses saved up, but for someone with a family,

9 to 12 months would be safer."

Arjun mentally calculates his monthly expenses and realizes that saving such an amount will take time. "That sounds like a huge sum," he says.

"It is," Eshwar acknowledges, "but you don't have to build it overnight. The key is to start small and be consistent."

Where Should You Keep It?

Arjun then asks the next logical question: "Where should I keep my emergency fund? Should I invest it somewhere?"

Eshwar shakes his head. "The purpose of an emergency fund is not to grow wealth, but to provide instant access to cash when needed. That means it should be kept in a safe, low-risk place with high liquidity."

Arjun thinks back to his past investment mistakes. "I once put some money into stocks thinking I could use it anytime, but then the market crashed, and I was stuck."

"That's why the stock market isn't a good place for emergency savings," Eshwar agrees. "Similarly, keeping all of it in a regular savings account is risky too—it's too easy to spend."

"So what's the best option?" Arjun asks.

"A liquid mutual fund or a fixed deposit with a sweep-in facility," Eshwar replies. "These options provide easy access to cash while ensuring that the money stays untouched until needed."

Arjun makes a mental note, realizing that financial security isn't just about earning more—it's also about managing risks wisely. With his new understanding, he is ready to take the next step in securing his financial future.

4. Sumant's Crisis Continues

Sumant had always prided himself on living life to the fullest. For him, financial stability was more about maintaining his image than securing his future. Despite facing job loss and mounting debts, he had not yet come to terms with the reality of his financial mismanagement. His habit of borrowing to fund his lifestyle had become second nature. However, life had a way of teaching hard lessons to those who refused to acknowledge them.

One evening, while driving home from a dinner outing with friends, Sumant's car broke down in the middle of a busy road. Frustrated, he stepped out and called for roadside assistance. The mechanic arrived, examined the car, and delivered the bad news—the repairs would cost

₹50,000. Sumant's heart sank. He had not anticipated such an expense, and worse, he had no savings to cover it.

As he stood there, feeling trapped, he instinctively reached for his phone to check his credit card limit. With a sigh of relief, he saw that he could still swipe his card and get the repairs done. Without thinking twice, he authorized the payment. Another ₹50,000 added to his already overburdened debt.

Later that night, as he sat alone, reviewing his financial situation, an overwhelming sense of helplessness washed over him. Every month, his salary barely covered his credit card EMIs, personal loan, and home loan. He had nothing left to save, and every new expense only pushed him deeper into the cycle of borrowing. He realized he was living paycheck to paycheck, with no safety net whatsoever. A sudden thought crossed his mind—what if something bigger happened? What if a medical emergency arose or another unexpected expense hit? How would he survive?

Desperate, he called Arjun the next morning. "Hey buddy, I need a favor," he started hesitantly. "My car broke down yesterday, and the repair cost drained me. I was wondering if you could lend me some money."

Arjun listened patiently but did not respond immediately. He had been in the same position once, but Eshwar's teachings had transformed his mindset. He took a deep breath and said, "Sumant, I understand how tough this must be for you. But if I give you money now, I won't be helping you—I'll only be delaying your realization."

Sumant frowned. "What do you mean? You know I'll return it once I get back on my feet."

Arjun's voice remained calm but firm. "I know you will, but that's not the point. You're trapped in a cycle of borrowing and spending, and the only way out is to change how you handle money. If I give you money today, you'll still be in the same situation tomorrow."

Sumant sighed heavily. "So, what do I do?"

Arjun leaned forward. "You need an emergency fund. You need to start setting aside money every month, even if it's a small amount, so you're never in this position again. When my mother fell sick, I didn't panic because I had an emergency fund. That's the difference between financial security and financial stress."

Sumant was silent for a moment. He had always dismissed the idea of saving for emergencies, believing that his income was enough to cover his needs. But now, standing at the edge of financial ruin, he realized how wrong he had been.

"I don't even know where to start," he admitted.

Arjun smiled. "That's the first step—acknowledging the problem. I'll help you, but not by giving you money. I'll show you how to build your emergency fund and get out of this debt trap."

For the first time in years, Sumant felt hopeful. Perhaps this was the turning point he had been unknowingly waiting for.

5. Arjun's Step-by-Step Plan to Build an Emergency Fund

Determined to secure his financial future, Arjun decided to follow Eshwar's advice systematically. He knew that financial stability wasn't built overnight—it required consistency, discipline, and a solid plan. So, he broke it down into clear steps.

Step 1: Calculating His Monthly Expenses

Arjun sat down and meticulously noted his monthly expenses. After careful assessment, he realized that his essential monthly costs, including rent, groceries, utilities, and transportation, added up to ₹50,000. This figure became his baseline for calculating his emergency fund target.

Step 2: Setting a Goal for His Emergency Fund

Following Eshwar's guidance, Arjun set his initial goal—to save at least six months' worth of living expenses. That meant accumulating ₹3 lakh. For the first time, he truly understood why this buffer was essential. It wasn't just a number; it was his financial safety net, ensuring he wouldn't have to rely on loans or credit cards during emergencies.

Step 3: Automating His Savings

Arjun realized that the easiest way to ensure consistency was to automate his savings. He set up a systematic investment plan (SIP) that directed ₹10,000 every month into a liquid mutual fund. By doing this, he eliminated the temptation to spend the money elsewhere. The key, he learned, was to make saving effortless and automatic.

Step 4: Choosing the Right Place to Store His Emergency Fund

Arjun debated where to keep his emergency savings. He knew that storing it in a regular savings account would expose him to the temptation of withdrawing it for non-emergencies. On the other hand, investing it in stocks would be risky, as markets fluctuate, and he needed this fund to remain stable. Finally, he settled on a liquid mutual fund—a low-risk, high-liquidity option that would ensure his money was safe but still accessible in case of need.

Step 5: Ensuring Discipline and Patience

Building an emergency fund required patience. It wasn't something he could achieve in a month or two. However, he remained disciplined, resisting the urge to divert these funds for vacations or other discretionary expenses. The mental shift was significant—he now viewed financial security as a priority rather than an afterthought.

The Journey to Financial Peace

Over the next 18 months, Arjun consistently contributed to his emergency fund. With every passing month, he felt a growing sense of control over his finances. When he finally reached his ₹3 lakh goal, he experienced a deep sense of relief. No longer did unexpected expenses cause him stress—he was prepared.

For the first time in his life, Arjun felt financially secure. He no longer lost sleep over potential financial setbacks. Instead, he had built a cushion that allowed him to face life's uncertainties with confidence. More importantly, he now had a system in place to continue growing his wealth beyond just emergency savings.

His journey had taught him a crucial lesson—true financial freedom isn't about earning more, but about managing what you have wisely.

And with this newfound wisdom, Arjun was ready to take on the next stage of his financial journey.

6. The Turning Point for Sumant

Sumant sat alone in his dimly lit apartment, the glow from his laptop screen reflecting on his weary face. The numbers on the screen told a story he no longer wanted to be part of—his credit card debt had ballooned, interest charges piling up like an unstoppable avalanche. The car repair had set him back another ₹50,000, and his savings were still at zero. His mind raced as he thought about his financial state.

For the first time, he wasn't just frustrated—he was exhausted.

He leaned back, exhaling sharply. *"How did I get here? How did Arjun manage to turn things around while I keep falling deeper?"* He knew the answer. Arjun had learned to plan ahead, while he had spent years reacting to problems as they came.

That night, unable to sleep, Sumant picked up his phone and scrolled through old messages with Arjun. His friend had changed. He was more confident, composed, and in control. Just a year ago, Arjun would have panicked over a sudden ₹50,000 expense—now, he barely flinched.

"What's stopping me from doing the same?"

The next morning, Sumant made a decision. He would no longer be a victim of his circumstances. He picked up the phone and called Arjun.

"Hey, buddy," Arjun greeted him, sensing something different in his tone.

"Arjun, I need to talk," Sumant said, his voice steady. "I need help, but not in the way I used to ask before. I want to change. Can you guide me?"

There was a pause before Arjun replied. "That's the first step, my friend. Let's get to work."

The First Challenge: Breaking Old Habits

Arjun invited Sumant over that evening. Sitting across from him, Arjun placed a pen and notepad in front of him. "Before we talk about solutions, let's diagnose the real problem," he said.

Sumant sighed. "I know the problem. I don't earn enough."

Arjun raised an eyebrow. "Really? Then how do you explain people who earn half your salary but still manage their finances better?"

Sumant frowned, but he knew Arjun was right. It wasn't about how much he earned—it was about how he spent.

Arjun continued, "You keep borrowing money because you don't have an emergency fund. You don't have an emergency fund because you never save. And you never save because you spend without thinking."

Sumant leaned forward, absorbing every word.

"Let's fix that. First, we need to get rid of the idea that you need a huge amount to start saving."

Sumant scoffed. "Easy for you to say. I'm drowning in debt. Where will I find extra money to save?"

Arjun grinned and handed him a blank sheet of paper. "Let's do the math."

Step 1: Identifying Wasteful Expenses

Together, they listed all of Sumant's monthly expenses. Rent, utilities, car loan EMI, food, fuel, entertainment, eating out, and so on.

"See this?" Arjun pointed at the restaurant bills. " ₹ 8,000 a month on eating out?"

Sumant winced. "I mean... yeah. But I need to eat."

"You need to eat, not eat out," Arjun corrected him. "And this— ₹3,000 on subscriptions?"

"Well, I use them sometimes..." Sumant mumbled.

Arjun circled several items in red. "I just found you an extra ₹12,000 per month without cutting anything essential. That's your emergency fund seed money right there."

Sumant's eyes widened. He had never looked at his expenses this way before.

Step 2: Automating Savings

Arjun continued, "Now that you've freed up ₹12,000, we'll put ₹5,000 toward your emergency fund and ₹ 7,000 toward clearing high-interest debt."

"Only ₹5,000? That'll take forever!" Sumant protested.

"That's the point," Arjun said. "We're focusing on consistency, not speed. If you try to save too much at once, you'll feel deprived and give up. Slow and steady wins this race."

They set up an automatic transfer— ₹5,000 every month into a liquid mutual fund. "This way, it's out of your hands before you can spend it," Arjun explained.

Sumant nodded. He was starting to see the bigger picture.

Step 3: Handling Financial Emergencies Without Borrowing

A month later, Sumant called Arjun in excitement. "Bro, my bike had a puncture, and guess what? I paid from my emergency fund instead of my credit card!"

Arjun laughed. "See? That's what financial security feels like."

Sumant was beginning to feel the difference. He was still in debt, but he was no longer helpless. He had a plan, and for the first time in years, he felt in control of his money.

The Final Test: Saying No to Borrowing

Three months into his financial transformation, Sumant faced a real test. His phone screen cracked, and the repair cost was ₹15,000. His old self would have swiped his credit card without a second thought. But this time, he paused.

He checked his emergency fund. There was ₹20,000 in it.

Instead of panicking, he calmly withdrew the amount and got his phone fixed. No loans, no stress.

When he told Arjun about it later, Arjun grinned. "You've changed, my friend. A year ago, this would've been another debt trap for you."

Sumant exhaled in relief. "Yeah. And it feels amazing."

Sumant's New Perspective on Money

Six months later, Sumant had saved ₹30,000 in his emergency fund. His debts were shrinking, and for the first time in his life, he felt financially secure.

"Arjun," he said over tea one evening, "I used to think rich people were just lucky. But now I realize—they just have a plan."

Arjun smiled. "Exactly. Wealth isn't about how much you earn. It's about how you manage it."

Sumant had finally understood the lesson. He wasn't waiting for emergencies to happen anymore—he was prepared for them. And that changed everything.

Key Takeaways on Building an Emergency Fund & Financial Transformation

1. The Importance of an Emergency Fund

- An emergency fund prevents financial disasters by covering unexpected expenses like medical bills, car repairs, or job loss.
- Relying on loans or credit cards for emergencies creates a debt trap.

2. How to Start an Emergency Fund

- Start small—don't wait for a big lump sum to save. Even ₹5,000 per month makes a difference.
- Identify unnecessary expenses (e.g., eating out, subscriptions) and redirect that money into savings.
- Automate savings by setting up a fixed amount to be transferred into a **liquid mutual fund or FD.**

3. Financial Discipline vs. Income Level

- High income alone does not guarantee financial security—**planning and discipline matter more.**
- Cutting unnecessary expenses can free up significant savings without affecting lifestyle essentials.
- Financially secure people don't just react to problems; they prepare for them.

4. The Right Place to Keep Your Emergency Fund

- Avoid keeping it in stocks (too risky) or a regular savings account (temptation to spend).

- A **liquid mutual fund** or a **fixed deposit (FD)** is ideal—easily accessible but not too tempting to spend.

5. Handling Financial Emergencies Without Borrowing

- Instead of taking loans, use your emergency fund to cover unexpected expenses.
- Train yourself to say **no** to unnecessary borrowing—even when facing sudden expenses.

6. The Power of Small, Consistent Steps

- Saving even a little every month leads to big results over time.
- Building an emergency fund takes time, but **the peace of mind it brings is priceless.**

CHAPTER SEVEN

The Power of Investing

The Realization: Savings Alone Won't Make You Rich

Arjun sat on his balcony, sipping his evening tea. The city skyline stretched before him, the orange hues of the sunset reflecting off the glass buildings. He felt a quiet sense of accomplishment. After months of disciplined effort, he had finally built his emergency fund—six months' worth of expenses, safely tucked away in a liquid mutual fund.

For the first time in his life, he felt financially secure. The constant fear of unexpected expenses no longer loomed over him. But despite this, a lingering worry remained in his mind.

"Is this enough?" he wondered.

That night, as he visited Eshwar, his mentor, the question weighed on him heavily.

"Eshwar Sir," Arjun said as he settled onto the old wooden chair in his mentor's study, "I've followed everything you told me. I've built my emergency fund, and I feel better than ever. But..." he hesitated.

"But what?" Eshwar asked, smiling knowingly.

"But I still feel uncertain about the future. What about retirement? What about my long-term goals? Will just saving money be enough?"

Eshwar chuckled softly and picked up a pen. He scribbled a number on a piece of paper and slid it across the table.

"Arjun, do you know what this is?"

Arjun leaned forward and read the number aloud. "6%... That's the current inflation rate, right?"

"Correct," Eshwar said. "Now tell me, what's the interest rate on your savings account?"

Arjun thought for a moment. "Around 3–4%."

Eshwar leaned back and raised an eyebrow. "So, tell me—if your money is growing at 3% but prices are rising at 6%, what's happening?"

Arjun stared at the paper, and the realization hit him like a wave.

"I'm actually losing money..." he murmured.

"Exactly!" Eshwar nodded. "People think saving is enough, but in reality, if your money isn't growing faster than inflation, you're falling behind every single year."

Arjun felt a tightness in his chest. He had spent so much time thinking that saving would secure his future. But now, he saw the truth.

"So, what should I do?" he asked.

Eshwar smiled. "You need to invest, my friend. Saving money protects you in the short term. But investing? That's what builds true wealth over time."

Arjun's curiosity was piqued. He had always thought of investing as something complex and risky. But now, for the first time, he was ready to learn.

2. Understanding the Magic of Compounding

The next evening, Arjun arrived at Eshwar's house with a notebook in hand. He was eager to learn but also nervous. Investing was something he had always associated with risk, speculation, and market crashes. His father used to warn him, "The stock market is like a casino—you either win big or lose everything." That fear had stayed with him for years.

But Eshwar had a way of making things simple.

"Arjun, today I'm going to teach you something that will completely change how you see money," Eshwar said as he pulled out his laptop.

He opened an Excel sheet and typed in a simple formula. "Before I explain, let me ask you something. Have you ever heard of the Rule of 72?"

Arjun shook his head. "No, what is it?"

"It's a quick way to calculate how long it takes for your money to double. You just divide 72 by the interest rate. Let me show you."

Eshwar typed in a new equation and turned the screen toward Arjun.

"Let's say you put ₹1 lakh in a savings account that gives you 3% interest per year. How long will it take to double?"

Arjun did the math in his head. "Seventy-two divided by three... that's 24 years!"

"Correct. Now, let's say you invest that same ₹1 lakh in a stock market fund that gives you 12% returns. How long will it take to double?"

"Seventy-two divided by twelve... just 6 years!"

Eshwar smiled. "Now, let's take it further. Suppose you start investing ₹10,000 every month in such a fund. Over 20 years, at 12% returns, how much do you think you'll have?"

Arjun grabbed his phone and opened the calculator. He quickly multiplied ₹10,000 by 12 months and then by 20 years.

"That's ₹24 lakhs," he said.

Eshwar chuckled. "That's the amount you've put in. But what about the compounding?" He turned the laptop screen to Arjun again. The number displayed on the screen made Arjun's jaw drop.

" ₹1.1 crore?!" Arjun exclaimed. "How?!"

Eshwar leaned back and sipped his tea. "That's the magic of compounding. When you invest, your money earns returns. Then those returns also start earning returns. The longer you let it grow, the more exponential the growth becomes."

Arjun's mind was racing. "So, if I wait for 25 years instead of 20, it will be even bigger?"

Eshwar nodded. "Yes. But now let me show you something even more shocking. What if you delay investing by just 5 years? Instead of 20 years, you invest for only 15 years."

Eshwar changed the numbers on the sheet, and Arjun saw the revised figure.

" ₹50 lakhs? That's half of what I would have had if I started 5 years earlier!"

"Exactly," Eshwar said, pointing at the screen. "This is what people don't realize. Every year you delay investing, you lose lakhs—even crores—of potential wealth."

Arjun was speechless. He had always thought of money in terms of what he could save. But now, he saw it in a completely different light.

"Sir, I've wasted so many years just saving instead of investing..."

Eshwar shook his head. "No, Arjun. The best time to start investing was ten years ago. The second-best time is today."

Arjun nodded with determination. "I want to start now. But where should I invest?"

Eshwar smiled. "That brings us to the next lesson—understanding different investment options."

3. The Different Investment Options

The next morning, Arjun was still thinking about what Eshwar had taught him. The power of compounding had opened his eyes. But now, a bigger question loomed in his mind—**Where should he invest?**

He had heard about fixed deposits, stocks, mutual funds, real estate, and even cryptocurrencies, but he had no idea which one was right for him.

Later that evening, he met Eshwar again. This time, he was prepared with questions.

"Eshwar sir, I understand that investing is important, but there are so many options. How do I know which one is right for me?"

Eshwar smiled. "That's a great question, Arjun. Investing is not just about choosing the highest-return option; it's about **balancing risk, liquidity, and growth potential**. Let's break down the major investment options one by one."

Eshwar picked up a whiteboard marker and wrote down five investment types.

a. Fixed Deposits & Bonds – Safe but Low Growth

"Many people in India love fixed deposits," Eshwar began. "It feels safe because the bank guarantees your money. But what most people don't realize is that it barely beats inflation."

Arjun nodded. "My father always told me to put money in FDs. But after what you told me about inflation, I see the problem. If inflation is 6% and an FD gives 5%, I'm actually losing money."

"Exactly," Eshwar said. "Fixed deposits and bonds are useful for **stability**, but they won't help you build wealth."

b. Real Estate – High Capital, Long-Term Returns

"Real estate is another favorite investment in India," Eshwar continued. "Property prices tend to increase over time, and you can earn rental income. But it requires big capital, and it's not always easy to sell when you need money."

Arjun thought for a moment. "So, real estate is good, but only if I have a lot of money and patience?"

"Correct. It's a great long-term investment but not ideal for someone just starting out with small capital."

c. Gold – Good for Stability, Not for Growth

"In India, gold has an emotional connection. People buy it for weddings and festivals. But as an investment, it doesn't generate income. It only appreciates over time."

Arjun frowned. "So gold is good for preserving wealth but not for growing it?"

"That's right," Eshwar confirmed. "It's useful as a hedge against inflation, but you shouldn't rely on it for wealth creation."

d. Stock Market – The Best Tool for Long-Term Wealth

"Now, here's where things get interesting," Eshwar said, his eyes lighting up. "The stock market has created more millionaires than any other investment. But most people fear it because they don't understand it."

Arjun leaned forward. "I've always heard that stocks are risky. People lose money all the time."

Eshwar laughed. "Let me ask you something. Have you ever heard of a shopkeeper who lost all his money because he **owned** a business?"

"No," Arjun replied. "If a business is good, it keeps making money."

"Exactly! Investing in stocks means you own a piece of a real business. If you choose strong companies, they grow over time, and so does your investment."

Arjun was intrigued. "And what about stock market crashes?"

"Great question," Eshwar said. "Crashes are **temporary**, but good businesses recover. The key is to invest in solid companies and hold them long-term."

e. Mutual Funds – The Beginner's Choice

"For people who don't have time to study stocks, mutual funds are a great option. A professional fund manager invests on your behalf, and you get diversification."

Arjun's eyes widened. "So, instead of buying one company's stock, I can invest in a mutual fund that holds multiple companies?"

"Exactly! Mutual funds reduce risk because your money is spread across different stocks."

Choosing the Right Investment

Eshwar turned to Arjun. "So, based on what we discussed, where do you think you should invest?"

Arjun thought for a moment. "Fixed deposits and bonds are safe but don't grow much. Real estate needs big capital. Gold is for stability, not growth. The stock market sounds like the best way to build wealth, and mutual funds are a good starting point."

Eshwar smiled. "You're catching on fast! The stock market is the best long-term wealth builder. But remember, it's not about **randomly buying stocks**. You need a strategy."

Arjun nodded. "I want to learn more about how to invest in stocks."

Eshwar leaned back. "That's exactly what we'll discuss next."

4. The Stock Market: A Wealth-Building Machine

Arjun felt a newfound excitement about investing. The idea that the stock market could generate long-term wealth fascinated him, but he was also cautious.

"Eshwar sir, I understand that investing in stocks can be rewarding. But if it's so good, why do people fear it so much?"

Eshwar chuckled. "Good question, Arjun. People fear what they don't understand. They hear stories of people losing money and assume the stock market is gambling. But let me ask you—why do businesses exist?"

"To make profits," Arjun replied.

"Exactly! And when you invest in stocks, you're not buying lottery tickets—you're **owning a part of a real business.** If the business grows, your investment grows too."

Arjun nodded, but another doubt lingered in his mind. "If it's that simple, why doesn't everyone invest in the stock market?"

Eshwar smiled and said, "Because most people don't have patience. They want quick money. But investing is like planting a tree—it takes time to grow, but once it does, it provides shade and fruits for years."

How Stocks Create Wealth

Eshwar took out his notepad and wrote down three key ways the stock market builds wealth:

1. Capital Appreciation – Stocks increase in value over time

"If you had invested   ₹10,000 in Infosys in the early 1990s, do you know how much it would be worth today?"

Arjun shook his head.

"Over ₹5 crores! That's the power of long-term investing."

Arjun was amazed. "But how does this happen?"

"When a company grows, its profits increase, and so does its stock price. If you invest in strong businesses, their value rises over time, making you wealthy."

2. Dividends – Companies share profits with investors

"Some companies distribute a part of their profits to shareholders as dividends. These can be reinvested to buy more shares, compounding your returns over time."

Arjun thought for a moment. "So, even if the stock price doesn't increase immediately, I can still earn money through dividends?"

"Exactly! A good dividend stock provides you with **passive income.**"

3. Power of Compounding – Reinvesting earnings accelerates growth

"Remember the example of ₹10,000 per month growing into ₹1 crore?"

Arjun nodded.

"That's compounding at work. Your money earns returns, those returns generate more returns, and the cycle continues."

The Stock Market vs. Other Investments

Eshwar decided to put things into perspective.

Investment	Annual Returns (Approx.)	Wealth Growth Over 20 Years (₹1 Lakh Invested)
Savings Account	3%	₹1.8 Lakhs
Fixed Deposit	5%	₹2.65 Lakhs
Gold	8%	₹4.66 Lakhs
Real Estate	10%	₹6.73 Lakhs
Stock Market (Nifty 50 Avg.)	12-15%	₹9.65–₹16.37 Lakhs

"Now you see why investing in stocks is the best way to build long-term wealth," Eshwar said.

Arjun looked at the table and finally understood. "The difference is huge! If I rely only on FDs or savings accounts, I'll never grow rich."

Eshwar nodded. "Correct. But remember, **knowledge is key**. Without understanding how the market works, investing can be dangerous."

Arjun's Fear: Is Stock Investing Gambling?

Arjun had another concern. "But sir, I've heard people say that the stock market is like a casino. Isn't it risky?"

Eshwar laughed. "Only for those who don't know what they're doing! Let me explain."

He took out his notepad again and wrote down:

Investing ≠ Trading – Traders buy and sell stocks frequently, but **investors hold quality stocks for the long term.**

Volatility ≠ Risk – "Short-term price movements don't matter if you're investing in strong businesses. A temporary dip is not a loss unless you sell in panic."

Market Crashes Are Opportunities – "Many people panic during market crashes, but smart investors buy stocks at low prices."

Arjun started seeing things differently. "So, it's not the market that is risky—it's the lack of knowledge that is dangerous?"

"Exactly!" Eshwar said. "The real risk is not understanding what you're investing in."

Arjun was beginning to see the stock market as an opportunity rather than a gamble.

5. The Misconceptions About Stock Market Investing

Arjun was beginning to see the stock market as a powerful tool for wealth creation. However, he still had doubts. He had heard too many horror stories about people losing money, going bankrupt, and regretting their investment decisions.

That evening, as he and Eshwar sat in the garden, Arjun decided to voice his concerns.

"Eshwar sir, I understand that investing is different from trading, but I still feel the stock market is risky. I've seen people lose huge amounts of money. Isn't it like gambling?"

Eshwar smiled, as if he had been expecting this question.

"Arjun, let's say you're driving on a highway. If you close your eyes and drive at full speed, what will happen?"

Arjun frowned. **"I'll crash, of course."**

"Exactly! Does that mean driving itself is dangerous? Or is it the reckless way of driving?"

Arjun thought for a moment. "It's the reckless driving that's dangerous."

"The stock market is the same. If you invest without understanding, without patience, and without a plan, you will crash. But if you follow principles, stay disciplined, and invest wisely, the stock market is one of the safest ways to build wealth."

Debunking the Common Myths About Investing

Eshwar could see that Arjun still had some hesitation. So, he decided to break down the most common misconceptions.

Myth #1: "Investing in stocks is the same as gambling."

Reality: Gambling is based on luck, while investing is based on knowledge.

"Gamblers bet on unpredictable outcomes. But investors analyze businesses, study financials, and make informed decisions," Eshwar explained.

Example: "Imagine you buy shares of a strong company like TCS or HDFC Bank. You are not betting—you are owning a part of a successful business."

Arjun nodded. **"So, the key difference is knowledge and strategy."**

Myth #2: "Stock prices are too volatile. I will lose all my money."

Reality: Volatility is normal, but temporary losses are not real losses unless you sell in panic.

Example: "During the 2008 market crash, many stocks fell by 50% or more. But investors who stayed invested made huge profits in the next decade."

"The stock market moves in cycles. Short-term fluctuations don't matter if you're invested in quality stocks for the long term."

Arjun was beginning to understand. "So, if I don't panic and hold on, I won't lose money?"

"Exactly! The only people who lose are those who sell in fear or invest in bad stocks without research."

Myth #3: "I need a lot of money to invest in stocks."

Reality: You can start with as little as ₹500.

Example: "If you invest just ₹5,000 per month in a good mutual fund, you can accumulate over ₹1 crore in 20 years."

"Investing is not about how much you have. It's about how early you start and how consistent you are."

Arjun smiled."This is a big relief! I always thought I needed lakhs to start investing."

Myth #4: "The market is manipulated by big players. Small investors always lose."

Reality: Long-term investors always win.

Example: "Even though big players influence short-term price movements, they cannot control the long-term success of great businesses. If you invest in strong companies, no one can take away your wealth."

"Do you think Reliance or Infosys became successful because of manipulation? No, they became successful because of their business performance."

Arjun was starting to see the truth. "So, if I invest wisely, I don't need to worry about these so-called big players?"

"Absolutely. You need to focus on long-term growth, not short-term noise."

6. Sumant's Get-Rich-Quick Mistake

Arjun was making steady progress in understanding stock market investing. However, not everyone around him was on the same path.

His friend, Sumant, was someone who always looked for shortcuts in life. Whether it was trying to get a promotion without putting in the effort or looking for ways to double his money overnight, Sumant believed that hard work was for fools. He had heard about the stock market and saw it as a "gold mine" waiting to be tapped.

One evening, Sumant rushed to Arjun's house, excitement radiating from his face.

"Arjun! I found a jackpot stock tip! This is my golden chance to become rich."

Arjun, who had been discussing investments with Eshwar for the past few weeks, immediately became cautious.

"What stock are you talking about?"

"It's called NovaTech Ltd. My office colleague's uncle works for a big investor, and he got inside information. The stock is about to double in a week! I'm putting in ₹1 lakh tomorrow."

Arjun's stomach tightened. "Sumant, have you researched the company? Do you know what they do?"

Sumant shrugged. "Who cares? I just need to buy and sell at the right time. If I wait and analyze, the opportunity will be gone!"

Arjun sighed. He could see that Sumant was blinded by greed.

He tried to reason with him. "Sumant, investing isn't about quick profits. If this stock were truly going to double in a week, don't you think everyone would already know? Please don't put your hard-earned money into something just because someone else told you to."

But Sumant was too excited to listen.

The next day, he bought 200 shares of NovaTech Ltd. at ₹500 per share.

What happened next was a disaster.

A few days later, instead of going up, the stock **crashed to ₹250 per share.** In a matter of days, Sumant's ₹1 lakh investment had shrunk to ₹50,000.

He panicked. **"What is happening? The stock was supposed to double!"**

He called his colleague, who had given him the tip, but the number was switched off.

Desperate, he called Arjun. "I've lost ₹50,000 in just a few days! I knew the stock market was a scam!"

Arjun sighed. "The stock market isn't a scam, Sumant. You just invested blindly without knowledge."

This was a painful but valuable lesson for Sumant. Many people enter the stock market with a get-rich-quick mindset and end up burning their fingers.

Why Most People Lose Money in the Stock Market

Eshwar, hearing about Sumant's mistake, decided to explain why people like him lose money.

1. They Chase Hot Tips

"Most people invest based on rumors and stock tips rather than real knowledge."

2. They Have No Patience

"They expect to double their money overnight instead of letting investments grow over time."

3. They Panic When Prices Fall

"A temporary drop makes them sell in fear, turning a paper loss into a real loss."

4. They Put All Their Money in One Stock

"If the stock crashes, their entire investment is wiped out."

5. They Have No Plan

"They don't set long-term goals and just buy randomly."

Sumant's mistake was a classic example of what **not** to do in the stock market.

7. Arjun's First Steps into Investing

While Sumant was regretting his mistake, Arjun decided to take a smarter approach. He knew he had to learn before investing.

The next day, he met Eshwar.

"Sir, I'm ready. How do I start investing the right way?"

Eshwar smiled, proud of Arjun's responsible attitude.

"Good. The first step is understanding the golden rules of investing."

Golden Rule #1: Invest Only What You Don't Need for 5+ Years

"Never invest money you need for immediate expenses. The stock market is best for long-term wealth creation."

Eshwar explained how successful investors think in terms of decades, not days.

Example:

"Imagine you had invested ₹1 lakh in Asian Paints in 2000. Today, that investment would be worth over ₹50 lakh. But you wouldn't have seen this growth overnight."

Golden Rule #2: Understand the Business Before Buying a Stock

"Would you buy a company without knowing what it does? Then why buy its stock without research?"

Eshwar gave another example.

Example:

"If you were going to start a restaurant, wouldn't you check the location, competitors, and quality of the chef? You must do the same when buying a stock."

Golden Rule #3: Avoid Speculation and Focus on Long-Term Growth

"Don't try to predict short-term price movements. Instead, invest in fundamentally strong companies and

hold them for years."

Eshwar then asked Arjun, "**How do you plan to start investing?**"

Arjun thought for a moment. "I want to start small, maybe with an index fund. Then, as I learn more, I'll invest in individual stocks."

Eshwar nodded in approval. "That's the best way to start!"

Arjun's First Investment

Instead of jumping in blindly like Sumant, Arjun took measured steps:

Step 1: Opened a Demat Account

"This was the gateway to buying stocks and mutual funds."

Step 2: Invested ₹5,000 in an Index Fund

"This gave him exposure to the entire market with low risk."

Step 3: Researched and Bought Two Blue-Chip Stocks

"He chose strong companies with proven business models."

For the first time in his life, Arjun felt **in control of his financial future.**

"This is not gambling. This is real wealth-building."

The Emotional Side of Investing

As Arjun started investing, he realized something surprising—investing wasn't just about numbers and logic.

It was an **emotional journey.**

Fear: When the market dropped, he felt uneasy. Should he sell?

Greed: When his stocks went up, he wanted to buy more.

Doubt: Was he making the right decisions?

He remembered what Eshwar had said earlier. **"The biggest enemy in investing is not the market. It is your own emotions."**

Arjun made a promise to himself: "I will invest with knowledge and discipline, not fear and greed."

Key Takeaways from This Chapter

- Avoid get-rich-quick schemes. They lead to losses.
- Investing is not gambling—it requires knowledge and patience.
- The best investors think in decades, not days.
- Your emotions will challenge you—stay disciplined.
- Start small, learn, and grow your investments wisely.

CHAPTER EIGHT

Mastering the Stock Market Mindset

1. The Biggest Challenge: Controlling Emotions

It had been a few months since Arjun made his first stock market investments. Initially, he felt excited. Seeing the prices of his stocks inching upward made him feel like he had made the right decisions. He logged into his brokerage account daily, sometimes multiple times a day, just to check the numbers.

Then, one day, something changed.

Arjun woke up as usual, checked his phone, and saw a **red screen flashing across the stock market app.**

Market Down 2.5%! Major Stocks Take a Hit

His heart started pounding. He quickly scrolled through his portfolio.

- **Stock A** – Down **8%**
- **Stock B** – Down 6%
- **Stock C** – Down **12%!**

His total portfolio had dropped by **10% overnight.**
"Oh no! Should I sell before it gets worse?"

He felt a wave of panic rush over him. What if the market kept crashing? What if his investments went to zero?

He called Eshwar immediately.

"Sir, my portfolio is down 10%! What should I do? Should I sell everything before it's too late?"

Eshwar chuckled on the other end. **"Ah, so now you are experiencing the real stock market, aren't you?"**

Arjun was confused. **"How can you be so calm? This is serious! My hard-earned money is disappearing!"**

There was a short pause before Eshwar replied, his voice calm and steady.

"Arjun, let me ask you something. If you own an apartment and tomorrow the property market falls by 10%, will you immediately sell your house in panic?"

Arjun frowned. "No, of course not! That would be foolish."

"Exactly. So why do you want to sell your stocks when they temporarily drop in price?"

Arjun went silent.

Eshwar continued, "Your biggest enemy in investing isn't the market—it's your emotions. The stock market tests your patience, discipline, and emotional control more than anything else. The real question isn't whether stocks go up or down—it's whether you can remain rational when things don't go as expected."

The Emotional Rollercoaster of Investing

Eshwar then explained something every investor faces—the emotional cycle of the stock market.

- **Euphoria:** When stocks rise, investors feel invincible. "I'm a genius! I should invest more!"

- **Anxiety:** When stocks fluctuate, investors start second-guessing. "Is this normal?"
- **Panic:** When the market falls, fear takes over. "I should sell before I lose everything!"
- **Hope:** When the market stabilizes, investors think, "Maybe things will be okay."

This cycle repeats over and over. Most people fail because they **buy during euphoria** and **sell during panic**—the exact opposite of what they should be doing.

Eshwar smiled. "The market is a game of patience. If you cannot control your emotions, you will always lose money, no matter how smart you are."

The Story of Two Investors: Who Wins?

To drive the lesson home, Eshwar shared a story.

Investor 1: The Emotional Investor (Ravi)

- Ravi started investing during a bull market when everything was rising.
- He felt confident and invested aggressively.
- The market suddenly fell, and panic set in. He sold everything at a loss.
- Later, when the market recovered, he regretted selling and bought again—but at higher prices.
- He kept repeating this cycle and **lost more than he gained.**

Investor 2: The Calm Investor (Deepak)

- Deepak invested steadily, regardless of the market conditions.
- When the market fell, he reminded himself, "This is temporary."

- Instead of selling, he bought more at lower prices.
- Over the years, his portfolio **grew significantly.**

Eshwar looked at Arjun and asked, **"Who do you want to be—Ravi or Deepak?"**

Arjun took a deep breath.

"I want to be like Deepak. But it's so hard to control emotions when I see my money disappearing."

Eshwar nodded. "It's natural. That's why the best investors have a system that protects them from their own emotions."

How to Control Your Emotions in Investing

Eshwar gave Arjun three practical strategies to handle emotions in the stock market:

1. Stop Checking Prices Daily

"If you check stock prices every day, you will always feel anxious. Look at your portfolio once a month or even once a quarter."

Actionable Tip: Set a rule—check your portfolio only on the first Monday of every month.

2. Have a Clear Investment Plan

"If you have a plan, you won't make impulsive decisions. Decide beforehand how much you will invest, in which stocks, and for how long."

Example: "I will invest ₹10,000 per month in blue-chip stocks for the next 5 years."

3. Think Like a Business Owner

"When you buy a stock, think of yourself as owning a part of the business. Do you sell your entire business because of one bad month? No! So don't do it with stocks."

Mindset Shift: Instead of thinking, *"The stock price is down,"* think *"Has the company's business really changed?"*

Arjun's Transformation

That night, Arjun reflected on everything Eshwar had said.

He realized that his biggest fear wasn't really losing money—it was **losing control**. But now, he understood that **market ups and downs are normal**.

The next morning, Arjun checked his portfolio one last time.

He saw the same red numbers, but this time, he **felt different**.

Instead of fear, he felt **prepared**.

He took a deep breath and whispered to himself, "**I am in this for the long run.**"

For the first time, Arjun **felt like a true investor.**

2. Understanding Market Cycles

The next time Arjun met Eshwar, he felt a lot calmer. The lessons on emotional control had given him a new perspective. However, there was still one lingering fear.

"Sir, even if I control my emotions, how do I know when to invest? What if I enter the market at the wrong time? Sometimes the market goes up, and sometimes it crashes. How do I handle that?"

Eshwar smiled. "Ah, now you are asking the right questions. To be a successful investor, you must understand market cycles. The stock market, just like nature, has seasons. If you recognize these patterns, you will never fear a market crash again."

The Four Market Cycles

Eshwar pulled out a chart from his bag.

Bear Market: Prices fall sharply, fear dominates, and most investors panic and sell.

Recovery Phase: The market stabilizes, smart investors start buying at lower prices.

Bull Market: Prices rise steadily, optimism returns, and people invest aggressively.

Peak and Decline: Euphoria sets in, stock prices are overvalued, and eventually, a crash happens.

"Markets move in cycles. Just like summer doesn't last forever, neither does winter. But those who prepare for both seasons thrive."

Arjun nodded. "So when stocks are crashing, it's like winter in the market?"

"Exactly. And what do you do in winter? You prepare for spring."

The Cycle of Investor Emotions

Eshwar showed another chart:

Optimism: "The market is doing well, I should invest more!"

Excitement: "I'm making great returns. I'm a genius!"

Euphoria: "Everyone is buying stocks! This will never go down!"

Anxiety: "Why are my stocks falling a little?"

Fear: "This is getting bad. Should I sell?"

Panic: "I'm losing everything! I must sell now!"

Despair: "I'll never invest again!"

Hope: "The market is stabilizing. Maybe it will recover."

Relief: "My portfolio is improving."

Optimism:*Cycle repeats...*

Eshwar leaned back and said, "Most people buy during euphoria and sell during panic. That's why they lose money. But if you understand these cycles, you will do the opposite—buy when others are fearful and sell when others are greedy."

The Biggest Market Crashes and Recoveries

To prove his point, Eshwar pulled out historical stock market data.

2008 Financial Crisis:

- The market crashed **50%**. Everyone panicked and sold.
- But those who stayed invested or bought at lower prices saw **massive profits** when the market recovered.

2020 COVID-19 Crash:

- The stock market fell nearly **40% in a month**.
- Many sold in fear, but within a year, the market reached **new all-time highs**.

What does this teach us?

"No matter how bad a crash seems, the market always recovers. Crashes are opportunities, not disasters."

Arjun was amazed. "So the secret is to stay calm and buy during market crashes?"

Eshwar nodded. "Yes, but only if you are investing in strong businesses. Crashes destroy weak companies but create wealth for those who invest wisely."

How Arjun Will Handle Market Cycles from Now On

Arjun now had a strategy:

During market crashes: Stay calm and look for opportunities to buy quality stocks at discounts.

During bull markets: Avoid getting carried away by greed.

During peak euphoria: Be cautious and don't invest blindly.

During recovery phases: Continue investing regularly.

For the first time, **he felt confident about handling market ups and downs.**

3. The Importance of a Long-Term Mindset

After understanding market cycles, Arjun felt more confident. He realized that stock prices move up and down in predictable patterns, but he still had one doubt.

"Sir, even if I understand these cycles, how do I know when to invest and when to sell? Should I wait for the next crash to buy? Or should I sell if I see signs of a peak?"

Eshwar chuckled. "Ah, the eternal question! Many investors spend their entire lives trying to time the market. But let me show you why that's a mistake."

Stock Market History and Long-Term Growth

Eshwar pulled out a long-term chart of the Indian stock market.

"Look at this chart of the NIFTY 50 index over the last 30 years. What do you notice?"

Arjun examined the chart. There were many dips—some small, some large. But over time, the overall trend was unmistakable. The market kept going higher.

"It always goes up in the long run!" Arjun exclaimed.

Eshwar nodded. "Exactly. The stock market rewards patient investors. Yes, there are crashes, but history has shown that the market always recovers and moves to new highs."

He continued, "For example, after the 2008 financial crisis, the Indian stock market lost nearly 60% of its value. People thought it was the end. But within a few years, it not only recovered but reached new highs. The same thing happened after the COVID-19 crash in 2020."

Arjun absorbed this carefully. "So the lesson is... never panic during crashes?"

Eshwar smiled. "Yes, but more importantly, never lose focus on the long-term picture."

Short-Term Thinking vs. Long-Term Thinking

Eshwar leaned forward and said, "Most people enter the stock market with the wrong mindset. They want to make quick money. They look at daily stock movements, they listen to news predictions, and they try to trade based on short-term trends."

He continued, "But the truth is, nobody can consistently predict short-term movements. Even professional fund managers with years of experience fail at it."

"But sir, why do so many people focus on short-term trading if it's so difficult?" Arjun asked.

"Because of greed," Eshwar answered. "People think they can outsmart the market. They want quick profits and don't have the patience to hold investments for years. But if you study the richest investors in the world—Warren Buffett, Rakesh Jhunjhunwala, PeterLynch—they all followed the same principle: long-term investing."

He then added, "In contrast, most short-term traders eventually lose money and quit."

Arjun thought about this for a moment. He had always seen advertisements about 'Making ₹10,000 daily from trading' or 'Turning ₹1 lakh into ₹10 lakhs in 3 months.'

Now, he understood the truth. Short-term trading was a trap for most people.

How Compounding Works Over Time

Eshwar grabbed his notebook and wrote:

₹1 lakh invested in a fixed deposit at 6% for 20 years = ₹3.2 lakhs

₹1 lakh invested in stocks at 15% for 20 years = ₹ 16.4 lakhs

Arjun's eyes widened. "That's a huge difference!"

Eshwar smiled. "Yes, and this is why you must stay invested for the long term. The longer your money stays in the market, the more it grows. This is called compounding."

He continued, "The stock market doesn't reward those who jump in and out. It rewards those who stay invested in great companies for years."

Arjun nodded. "Now I understand why long-term investing is the real secret to wealth."

Patience Pays Off

Eshwar leaned back and said, "Now tell me, if you invest in a fundamentally strong company, does it matter if its stock price falls 10% next month?"

Arjun shook his head. "No, because I know the company will grow over time, and my investment will increase in value."

Eshwar clapped his hands. "Now you're thinking like a real investor!"

He continued, "Many people sell stocks out of fear when prices drop. But smart investors see it as an opportunity to buy more at a discount. If you trust your research and hold onto great companies, time will do the rest of the work for you."

How Arjun Will Invest from Now On

Arjun made a commitment to himself:

He will invest in strong businesses, not short-term trends.

He will hold his investments for the long term.

He will ignore daily stock market noise and focus on company fundamentals.

He finally understood what Eshwar had been trying to teach him:

The stock market is a tool to build long-term wealth—not a place for quick gambling.

4. The Mistake of Timing the Market

After learning the importance of long-term investing, Arjun felt more confident. However, one question still lingered in his mind.

"Eshwar sir, if the market always recovers and grows over time, wouldn't it be better to wait for a crash and invest when prices are low? That way, I can buy at the lowest price and maximize my returns."

Eshwar smiled. "Arjun, this is a common thought among investors. In theory, it sounds logical. But in reality, it rarely works."

Arjun looked confused. "Why not? If I wait for a correction, I can enter at a cheaper price."

Eshwar picked up his phone and searched for past news headlines. He then turned the screen towards Arjun.

"Look at these news articles from the past. In 2016, experts predicted that the Indian stock market would crash due to global instability. It didn't happen. In 2018, analysts warned that valuations were too high, yet the market kept rising. In 2020, after the COVID-19 crash, many said the recovery was temporary. But within a year, the market had doubled."

Arjun was surprised. "So experts get it wrong too?"

"Not just sometimes—most of the time," Eshwar replied. "Even seasoned fund managers with decades of experience struggle to predict market tops and bottoms. If they can't do it consistently, do you think an average investor can?"

Arjun hesitated. "But surely some people succeed, right?"

"Yes, but it's mostly luck," Eshwar explained. "A few people may predict a crash correctly once or twice, but doing it consistently over a lifetime is nearly impossible. And while they wait for a perfect entry, the market keeps rising, leaving them behind."

The Risk of Staying Out of the Market

Eshwar took out a printed chart showing the performance of the NIFTY 50 over the past 20 years.

"Arjun, let's assume you had   ₹1 lakh to invest in the index in 2003. If you had stayed invested without trying to time the market, your investment would have grown to over   ₹15 lakhs by now."

Arjun's eyes widened. "That's impressive!"

"Now, let's assume you tried to time the market and missed just the 10 best trading days—days when the index had its biggest gains. Your returns would be cut in half."

Arjun leaned forward. "Just missing 10 days could make such a difference?"

"Yes, and if you missed the 20 best days, your returns would be even lower. The best days often come right after the worst days. People who panic and stay out of the market miss these rapid recoveries."

Arjun thought about it. "So, instead of trying to time the market, I should just invest regularly and stay invested?"

"Exactly," Eshwar said. "That's why smart investors use a strategy called SIP—Systematic Investment Plan."

Why Systematic Investment Works

Eshwar explained how investing a fixed amount every month in mutual funds or stocks reduces the risk of market fluctuations.

"When prices are high, your money buys fewer units. When prices are low, your money buys more units. Over time, this balances out your purchase cost, and you don't have to worry about timing the market."

Arjun nodded. "So, instead of waiting for a crash, I should just keep investing consistently."

"Yes. Think of it like planting a tree. If you wait for the perfect weather, you may never plant it. But if you start today and nurture it regularly, it will grow into something strong over time."

Arjun smiled. "That makes sense. I'll stop worrying about perfect timing and focus on long-term investing."

Eshwar patted him on the back. "That's the right mindset."

Arjun was finally overcoming one of the biggest mistakes new investors make—waiting for the perfect moment instead of taking action.

Now, he was ready to learn another crucial lesson: the danger of following stock market tips from unreliable sources.

5. The Danger of Following Hot Tips

One evening, while Arjun was analyzing his stock portfolio, his phone buzzed with a message from one of his college friends, Rakesh.

"Check out ABC Industries! My broker says it's about to hit the roof. Get in before it's too late!"

Arjun smirked. He had received similar messages before. But this time, he was more cautious.

A few minutes later, his phone rang again. It was Sumant.

"Arjun! I finally found a way to make quick money in the market," Sumant said excitedly.

Arjun sighed. "Let me guess, a stock tip?"

"Yes! A colleague of mine has inside information. This stock is going to double in a few weeks. I'm putting all my savings into it."

Arjun shook his head. "Sumant, we've talked about this before. Stock tips are dangerous. Did you research the company?"

Sumant brushed him off. "Why waste time on research when someone already did it for me? This is a once-in-a-lifetime chance!"

Arjun felt uneasy. But Sumant was too excited to listen.

The Trap of Greed

A few weeks later, Arjun met Sumant at a café. His friend's cheerful face had been replaced with frustration.

"Lost a fortune," Sumant muttered.

Arjun leaned forward. "What happened?"

"The stock didn't go up. It crashed! Turns out, the so-called insider information was just a pump-and-dump scheme. The promoters hyped the stock, and when people like me jumped in, they sold everything. Now it's worthless."

Arjun shook his head. "I warned you, Sumant. You can't rely on tips and speculation. Real investing isn't about chasing rumors—it's about strategy and patience."

Sumant sighed. "I wanted a shortcut. I didn't realize that the stock market punishes greed."

Arjun nodded. "That's why Eshwar sir always says, 'If a stock tip sounds too good to be true, it probably is.'"

Sumant leaned back. "So, what now?"

"Now," Arjun said, "you learn how to invest the right way. No more gambling. No more blind bets."

For the first time, Sumant seemed ready to listen. And Arjun knew this was an important step—not just for his friend, but for himself as an investor.

6. Developing an Investor's Mindset

The next Sunday, Arjun and Sumant met Eshwar at his home. This time, Sumant was eager to learn rather than argue.

"I've realized that I don't know anything about investing," Sumant admitted. "How do I change that?"

Eshwar smiled. "The first step to becoming a successful investor is to develop the right mindset. The stock market isn't just about numbers; it's about psychology. Let's talk about the four essential traits every investor must cultivate."

Patience – Wealth Takes Time to Grow

Eshwar placed a small pot on the table. A tiny sapling was growing inside.

"Tell me, Sumant," he asked, "if you wanted this plant to grow into a large tree, what would you do?"

Sumant thought for a moment. "I'd water it regularly, make sure it gets sunlight, and wait."

"Exactly," Eshwar said. "Investing is the same. You can't expect results overnight. Just like this plant, your investments need time to grow. If you keep digging up the soil to check the roots, you'll kill the plant before it matures. The same happens when investors panic and sell too soon."

Sumant nodded. "I think that's what I've been doing—expecting quick returns and giving up when things go wrong."

Arjun added, "I guess that's why successful investors stay invested for years. They let time work in their Favor."

Discipline – Stick to Your Investment Plan

Eshwar took out a diary and showed them a page filled with notes. "This is my investment plan. I write down my goals, how much I'll invest each month, and the rules I follow. No matter what happens in the market, I stick to my plan."

Sumant raised an eyebrow. "Rules? What kind of rules?"

"For example," Eshwar explained, "I don't invest based on emotions. If a stock price suddenly drops, I don't panic and sell. If a stock I like is overvalued, I wait instead of rushing in. Investing without discipline is like driving without brakes—you're bound to crash."

Arjun looked at Sumant. "I think your mistake was not having a plan at all. You jumped in and out of stocks based on impulse."

Sumant sighed. "Guilty as charged. From now on, I'll follow a structured approach."

Emotional Control – Avoid Greed and Fear

Eshwar leaned back in his chair. "There's a saying in the market: 'The best investors are like monks—they don't let emotions control them.'"

Sumant laughed. "I'm the opposite of that. I get excited when prices go up and scared when they drop."

"That's exactly what you need to change," Eshwar said. "Most investors fail because they buy when they feel greedy and sell when they feel fearful. But the best opportunities often come when everyone else is scared."

Arjun remembered a story he had read. "Warren Buffett says, 'Be fearful when others are greedy, and greedy when others are fearful.'"

Eshwar nodded. "That's the mindset of a true investor. Control your emotions, and you'll avoid the biggest mistakes."

Continuous Learning – The Market Evolves, and So Should You

Eshwar got up and walked to his bookshelf, picking out a few books. He handed them to Sumant.

"These books will teach you how the market works. Investing isn't something you learn once and forget. The best investors keep learning, even after decades."

Sumant flipped through one of the books. "I never thought of investing as something you have to study."

"That's the difference between a gambler and an investor," Eshwar said. "One relies on luck, the other on knowledge."

Arjun smiled. "That reminds me of what you told me earlier, sir—'Ignorance is the real risk, not the stock market.'"

Sumant took a deep breath. "Alright. I'm ready to start fresh. No more gambling, no more shortcuts. I want to do this the right way."

Eshwar patted his shoulder. "Good. If you master these four traits—patience, discipline, emotional control, and continuous learning—you won't just become a better investor. You'll become a wiser person."

For the first time in a long while, Sumant felt hopeful. And Arjun, too, realized that investing wasn't just about money—it was about developing the right mindset for life.

Key Takeaways from this Chapter:

1. **Your emotions are your biggest enemy in investing –** Fear and greed lead to bad decisions. Learning to control emotions is the first step to success.

2. **Markets move in cycles –** Just like seasons, bull and bear markets come and go. Understanding this helps avoid panic selling or reckless buying.

3. **Think long-term –** Short-term market fluctuations don't matter if you are investing in strong businesses. The market has always recovered from crashes.

4. **You cannot time the market –** Even experts fail at predicting tops and bottoms. The best approach is to invest regularly and consistently.

5. **Avoid following hot stock tips –** Relying on rumors or quick-profit promises often leads to losses. Research and strategy are more important than luck.

6. **Patience is key –** Wealth grows over time, just like a tree. Constantly checking stock prices or making impulsive changes can harm your investments.

7. **Discipline matters –** A structured investment plan prevents emotional decisions and ensures steady financial growth.

8. **Emotional control separates winners from losers –** Successful investors don't get carried away by market euphoria or crash-driven fear.

9. **Continuous learning is necessary –** The stock market evolves, and so should investors. Reading books, studying successful investors, and understanding market trends are crucial for long-term success.

10. **Investing is not gambling –** A well-thought-out strategy based on knowledge and research will always outperform luck-based decisions.

By mastering these principles, one can not only succeed in the stock market but also develop a mindset that benefits other aspects of life.

CHAPTER NINE

Passive Income & Financial Independence

The Key to True Freedom

The cool evening breeze rustled through the trees as Arjun and Eshwar sat on a park bench, watching the sun dip below the horizon. The golden hues reflected in the lake before them, a picture of serenity—yet Arjun's mind was restless.

"Eshwar," Arjun said, breaking the silence, "I've started investing. I've learned to control my emotions. I know how to analyze stocks. But there's one thing I still don't understand…" He hesitated, as if unsure how to phrase his thoughts.

Eshwar smiled knowingly. "Go on, Arjun. What's bothering you?"

Arjun sighed. "I keep thinking… what's the end goal? I mean, sure, investing is great, but how do I ensure financial security for life? How do I reach a point where I never have to worry about money again?"

Eshwar leaned back, gazing at the sky as if searching for the right words. Then, he turned to Arjun with a glint of wisdom in his eyes.

"The goal, my boy, is to make money work for you so that you don't have to work for money."

Arjun frowned slightly. "But isn't that what investing does?"

Eshwar chuckled. "Yes, but investing is just a tool. The real key to freedom is something bigger—Passive Income."

Arjun's curiosity was piqued. "Passive income?"

Eshwar nodded. "It's money that flows into your pocket without requiring your constant effort. Imagine waking up in the morning, checking your bank account, and finding that you've earned money while you were asleep. That's true financial freedom, Arjun."

Arjun leaned forward, intrigued but skeptical. "That sounds amazing. But... is it really possible? Or is it just another dream people chase?"

Eshwar's expression turned serious. "It's not just possible, Arjun. It's necessary. If you ever want to break free from the rat race, you **must** build passive income streams. Otherwise, you'll spend your whole life working for money instead of letting money work for you."

A sudden realization hit Arjun. All his life, he had seen people working tirelessly—his father, his uncles, his colleagues. They earned well, but they never stopped working. Retirement was something they dreaded because it meant no income.

"But how do I build passive income?" Arjun asked eagerly.

Eshwar smiled. "Patience, my young friend. Let's start by understanding the difference between **active** and **passive** income."

Active vs. Passive Income

The next morning, Arjun met Eshwar at their usual coffee shop. The aroma of freshly brewed coffee filled the air as they settled into a corner booth.

Arjun, still reflecting on their conversation from the previous evening, wasted no time. "Alright, Eshwar, tell me—what exactly is passive income? And how is it different from what I earn now?"

Eshwar took a slow sip of his coffee before responding. "Let me ask you this—how do you make money right now?"

Arjun shrugged. "My salary, of course. I work every day, and at the end of the month, I get paid."

"Exactly." Eshwar leaned forward. "That, my friend, is **active income**. You trade your time and effort for money. The moment you stop working, the income stops."

Arjun frowned. He had never thought of it that way before. "So, passive income is...?"

Eshwar set down his cup. "Income that doesn't stop when you stop working. It's money that flows in whether you lift a finger or not."

Arjun's brows furrowed. "That sounds too good to be true. If it were that easy, why isn't everyone doing it?"

Eshwar chuckled. "Because most people don't know how. Or worse, they do know but never act on it. They're trapped in the mindset that they must work harder and harder to earn more, instead of making their money work for them."

Arjun was still skeptical. "Give me an example."

Eshwar leaned back and tapped his fingers on the table. "Alright, let's say two men, Raj and Sameer, both earn ₹ 1,00,000 a month. Raj spends everything—his salary is his lifeline. If he stops working tomorrow, he's broke. That's active income.

Now, Sameer is smarter. He saves and invests a portion of his earnings into dividend-paying stocks. Over time, these investments grow and start generating ₹20,000

per month in dividends. Even if Sameer stops working, he still earns that ₹20,000. The more he invests, the bigger his passive income becomes. One day, it might even surpass his salary."

Arjun's eyes widened. "So, he could eventually stop working and still make money?"

Eshwar nodded. "Bingo. That's financial freedom."

Arjun exhaled slowly, letting the idea sink in. He had always thought of work as the only way to earn money. The idea of creating **a system where money flows in without effort** felt... liberating.

"Okay," Arjun said, his mind racing with possibilities. "So, how do I build passive income?"

Eshwar smiled. "There are many ways. But let's start with one of the simplest—**dividends.**"

The Power of Dividends

Arjun sat back in his chair, rubbing his chin as he processed everything Eshwar had just told him. The concept of passive income had already started reshaping his understanding of financial security, but something about dividends felt particularly fascinating.

"So, dividends," Arjun said, leaning forward, "are basically free money?"

Eshwar chuckled. "That's one way to put it, but it's not entirely accurate. Dividends are a share of the company's profits. When you buy a stock, you're becoming a part-owner of the business. If the company does well, it rewards its shareholders by paying out a portion of its profits."

Arjun's eyes gleamed with curiosity. "That's interesting. So, how do I know which companies pay dividends?"

Eshwar picked up a pen and started sketching a simple example on a napkin. "Let's break it down. Say you invest in a company that declares a dividend of ₹10 per share.

If you own **1,000 shares**, you'll receive   ₹10,000 in dividend payments." He pushed the napkin toward Arjun.

Arjun's eyebrows lifted. "   ₹10,000? Just like that?"

Eshwar nodded. "Yes. And here's the best part—many good companies increase their dividends every year. That means if you keep holding those shares, your payouts can grow without you investing any extra money."

Arjun frowned slightly. "But wait... if the company is paying out its profits, doesn't that mean it has less money to grow?"

Eshwar smiled, impressed by Arjun's thought process. "That's exactly why not all companies pay dividends. Some reinvest their profits to expand the business. But well-established companies—ones that don't need to reinvest all their earnings—often reward shareholders through dividends."

Arjun thought for a moment, then smirked. "So basically, these companies are like generous landlords who pay rent to their shareholders?"

Eshwar laughed. "A creative way to put it! Yes, dividends are like rent payments from companies to their owners. The difference is, you don't have to maintain a building or deal with tenants."

Arjun's mind was already racing. He had spent the last few years trying to build wealth, always thinking that stock prices alone determined success. But now, he was seeing an entirely new perspective—one where money flowed to him without requiring constant effort.

"But how do I find the right dividend stocks?" Arjun asked. "What if a company pays a high dividend but is actually in trouble?"

Eshwar leaned back, folding his arms. "That's a smart question. Some companies lure investors by offering extremely high dividends, but if their business isn't strong, they might not sustain those payouts. That's why we don't just chase high yields—we look at consistency. A good dividend-paying company has a long history of **regular and increasing dividends**, stable cash flow, and strong financial health."

Arjun exhaled, realizing that even passive income required strategy. "Alright," he said, nodding. "I like this. Steady income, less stress."

Eshwar tapped his pen on the table. "And here's a secret weapon—**dividend reinvestment.** Instead of taking the cash, you can use your dividends to buy more shares. This means your stock holdings grow over time, and so does your future dividend income. It's like planting a money tree and using its fruit to grow more trees."

Arjun grinned. "So if I keep reinvesting, my income keeps compounding?"

"Exactly," Eshwar said. "This is why long-term investors love dividends. Many wealthy individuals live entirely off their dividend income without ever selling their stocks."

A spark ignited in Arjun's mind. "This is how you do it, right?" he asked, narrowing his eyes. "This is how you've built your wealth."

Eshwar's lips curled into a knowing smile. "Let's just say I haven't worried about my monthly expenses in years."

Arjun sat back, his mind buzzing with possibilities. Passive income wasn't just a concept—it was a way to escape financial insecurity forever. With every dividend-paying stock he held, he could inch closer to complete freedom.

He was about to ask his next question when Eshwar raised a hand. "Before we go deeper into stock selection, let's explore another source of passive income—one that's even older than dividends."

Arjun raised an eyebrow. "What's that?"

Eshwar's smile widened. "**Real estate.**"

Real Estate as an Income Source

Arjun stretched his arms, still digesting everything he had learned about dividends. The idea of money flowing into his account without lifting a finger was exhilarating. But as much as he liked the concept, something still nagged at him.

"Eshwar," he said, shifting in his chair, "dividends sound great, but stock prices can go up and down. What if a company stops paying dividends? Isn't there something more stable?"

Eshwar nodded, as if expecting the question. "That's where real estate comes in," he said, his voice carrying a hint of excitement. "Unlike stocks, which exist on paper, real estate is something tangible. You can see it, touch it, and—most importantly—earn from it in multiple ways."

Arjun smirked. "You mean like those guys who buy flats and rent them out?"

"Exactly," Eshwar said. "But let me show you why real estate is more than just collecting rent."

He picked up a pen and started drawing a simple diagram on a notepad:

Case Study: The Power of Rental Income

1. Buying a Property: Suppose you buy a flat for ₹50 lakh. You take a loan for ₹40 lakh and pay ₹10 lakh as a down payment.

2. Earning from Rent: You rent it out for ₹20,000 per month.

3. Loan Repayment: Your EMI is around ₹30,000, but the rent covers most of it.

4. Appreciation: Over time, the property value rises. In 10 years, it's worth ₹1 crore.

Arjun's eyes widened. "Wait a minute... so the tenant is helping pay off the loan?"

Eshwar smiled. "Exactly! That's the beauty of it. In a few years, your loan is gone, and now the rent becomes pure profit. Meanwhile, the property's value keeps increasing."

Arjun's fingers drummed on the table. "So, let me get this straight. I invest once, tenants pay for most of it, and later, I have an asset that gives me steady cash flow?"

Eshwar nodded. "And unlike stocks, which fluctuate daily, property prices are generally stable over the long run. If chosen wisely, real estate becomes a **reliable wealth-building machine.**"

Arjun was intrigued but frowned slightly. "But what about maintenance? Tenants can be a headache, right?"

Eshwar chuckled. "That's true. There are challenges—vacancy periods, maintenance costs, and tenant issues. But if you plan well, the rewards outweigh the risks."

Arjun nodded slowly, deep in thought. "I like it... but real estate needs a lot of money upfront. Not everyone has ₹50 lakh lying around."

Eshwar leaned forward. "That's why there's another option—one where you don't need to buy property but still earn rental income."

Arjun's head tilted in curiosity. "And what's that?"

Eshwar grinned. "**REITs—Real Estate Investment Trusts.**"

Digital Income Streams & REITs – Making Passive Income Accessible to Everyone

Arjun leaned forward, intrigued by Eshwar's last words. "REITs? Never heard of them. What are they?"

Eshwar smiled, sensing Arjun's curiosity. "A **Real Estate Investment Trust (REIT)** is like a mutual fund, but instead of stocks, it invests in real estate properties—malls, office buildings, warehouses, and even apartment complexes."

Arjun raised an eyebrow. "So, I can invest in real estate... without actually buying property?"

"Exactly," Eshwar nodded. "With REITs, you don't need crores to buy a property. You can start with as little as ₹ 5,000. These trusts own and manage real estate, and the rent they collect is distributed as dividends to investors like you."

Arjun's eyes lit up. "So, I can get rental income without worrying about tenants, maintenance, or paperwork?"

Eshwar chuckled. "That's the beauty of it. REITs give you the benefits of real estate without the hassle. Plus, they're liquid—you can sell your REIT shares anytime, unlike physical property, which takes months to sell."

Arjun nodded, absorbing this new information. "I never thought of real estate this way. So, if someone wants passive income but doesn't have huge capital, REITs are a good start?"

"Absolutely," Eshwar affirmed. "And there are more ways to earn passive income, especially in the digital world."

Arjun's curiosity deepened. "Like what?"

Eshwar leaned back, a knowing smile on his face. "Let's talk about digital income streams—opportunities that didn't exist a decade ago but are now making people financially free."

The Rise of Digital Income Streams

Eshwar took out his tablet and pulled up a few examples. "With technology, anyone can build passive income streams online. Here are some of the most popular ways."

1. Index Funds & ETFs – The Ultimate 'Set-and-Forget' Investment

- Instead of picking individual stocks, you invest in a basket of stocks that track an index like the NIFTY 50 or SENSEX.
- Since markets generally rise over time, this is a stress-free way to build wealth passively.
- "It's like buying the entire market instead of guessing which company will win," Eshwar explained.

Arjun nodded. "So, I don't have to research individual stocks, and I still make money?"

"Exactly. It's a favorite strategy for people who don't have time to actively manage investments."

2. Writing a Book or Creating an Online Course

- "Have you ever noticed how authors and course creators keep making money long after their work is done?" Eshwar asked.
- Arjun thought about it. "Yeah, once a book is written or a course is recorded, people keep buying it."
- "That's passive income," Eshwar said. "If you write an eBook, you earn every time someone buys it. The same goes for an online course."
- Arjun scratched his chin. "But not everyone is a writer or teacher."
- "True, but everyone has knowledge or skills someone else is willing to pay for."

3. Affiliate Marketing & Blogging

- "Ever clicked on a YouTube video where the creator says, 'Check out the link below'?" Eshwar asked.
- Arjun laughed. "Yeah, they always promote something."
- "That's affiliate marketing. They earn a commission when someone buys through their link."
- "So, you don't need to create a product—just promote others' products?"
- "Exactly. Many bloggers and YouTubers make lakhs every month just from affiliate commissions."

4. YouTube & Digital Content Creation

- Eshwar pointed to his phone. "You watch YouTube, right?"
- Arjun nodded. "Of course."
- "Every YouTuber earns from ad revenue, sponsorships, and memberships. Once their videos are uploaded, they keep making money without doing anything extra."
- "So, if someone has a YouTube channel that keeps growing, they can earn forever?"
- "Correct. It's digital real estate—the more content you own, the more passive income you generate."

Arjun's Lightbulb Moment

Arjun sat back, rubbing his chin. "I never realized there were so many ways to make money without actively working for it. Stocks, real estate, digital content... it's like a whole new world."

Eshwar grinned. "And this is just the beginning. Financial independence isn't about working harder—it's about working smarter. The more passive income you build, the sooner you'll reach true freedom."

Arjun's mind was racing with possibilities. He had always thought financial success meant climbing the corporate ladder, but now he saw a different path—one where his money worked for him instead of the other way around.

But there was still one question left. **How much passive income did he actually need to be financially free?**

Achieving Financial Independence – How Much Is Enough?

Arjun felt his mind buzzing with possibilities. Passive income wasn't just a concept anymore—it was a real, achievable goal. But one question kept nagging him.

He turned to Eshwar. "All of this makes sense, but... how do I know when I've made enough? How do I know when I'm financially free?"

Eshwar smiled knowingly. "Good question, Arjun. Tell me, how much do you spend every month?"

Arjun thought for a moment. "Around ₹1,00,000."

Eshwar nodded. "And what happens if you stop working today?"

Arjun hesitated. "Well... I'd have to rely on my savings. If I don't earn, I can't sustain my lifestyle for long."

"Exactly," Eshwar said. "That's because you still depend on active income. But what if your passive income covered all your expenses?"

Arjun's eyes widened. "That means... I wouldn't need to work at all."

"Bingo." Eshwar picked up a piece of paper and wrote down a simple formula:

Financial Freedom Number = Monthly Expenses × 12 ÷ Safe Withdrawal Rate

He explained, "Let's say your expenses are ₹1,00,000 per month. That's ₹12,00,000 per year. If you invest in assets that generate an average return of 6-8% per year, you'll need roughly ₹2-3 **crore** in investments to cover your expenses indefinitely."

Arjun stared at the numbers. "So if I build a portfolio of ₹2-3 crore, I can stop working and still live the same lifestyle?"

"Yes," Eshwar confirmed. "At that point, your money works for you. Whether you wake up and work or spend the day at the beach, your lifestyle doesn't change."

Arjun took a deep breath. It felt like a door had opened—a door to a life where he wasn't trapped in the cycle of earning and spending.

"But it's not just about the number," Eshwar continued. "It's about freedom. The freedom to do what you love, the freedom to choose how you spend your time, and the freedom to never worry about money again."

For the first time in his life, Arjun felt like he was in control of his future. Not just surviving—**but truly living.**

Sumant's Wake-Up Call

Just then, Sumant walked in. He had been overhearing the conversation. His face was tense, a stark contrast to Arjun's newfound excitement.

"I wish I had known all this earlier," Sumant muttered. "I've spent years running after promotions, working extra hours, and still, I feel stuck."

Arjun looked at his friend. "It's not too late, Sumant. You can start now."

Sumant shook his head. "I've only saved a small amount. I never thought about passive income."

Eshwar placed a reassuring hand on Sumant's shoulder. "The best time to start was ten years ago. The second-best time is today. You may have wasted time, but you don't have to waste your future."

Sumant swallowed hard. He had always assumed wealth meant a bigger paycheck. Now, he realized it was about **making money without working for it.**

For the first time in years, he felt hopeful.

Arjun's Final Goal

As they walked out of the café, Arjun turned to Eshwar.

"So, my goal is clear—build passive income, invest in the right assets, and achieve financial freedom."

Eshwar smiled. "Exactly. And when your passive income covers your expenses, you'll be free. No boss, no deadlines—just the life you choose to live."

Arjun clenched his fists. He was halfway there. **Now, nothing could stop him.**

Sumant's Wake-Up Call

It had been a while since Sumant and Arjun had sat down together for a heart-to-heart conversation. Lately, Sumant had been distant, consumed by his work and financial struggles. But tonight, as he met Arjun for dinner, he couldn't hide his frustration any longer.

As they settled into their seats, Sumant sighed heavily. "Man, I don't understand... I work longer hours than you, I've been in my job for years, and yet, I feel like I'm stuck in the same place. Meanwhile, you seem so... relaxed. Almost as if money isn't a concern for you anymore."

Arjun smiled. "That's because it isn't."

Sumant furrowed his brows. "How? How did you build wealth so fast? What's your secret?"

Arjun leaned back and chuckled. "It's not about working harder, Sumant. It's about making money work for you."

Sumant gave him a puzzled look. "What do you mean?"

Arjun leaned forward. "Think about it. You and I both started our careers around the same time. You focused on earning a salary, saving a little, and spending the rest. But

I focused on building **passive income.** I invested in stocks, dividends, and other income-generating assets. Now, my money grows even when I sleep."

Sumant's face darkened as the realization sank in. "So... all these years, I've been doing it wrong?"

Arjun shook his head. "Not wrong, just incomplete. Relying only on your salary means you're trading time for money. The moment you stop working, the income stops. But passive income? That keeps flowing whether you work or not."

Sumant ran his hands through his hair, frustration evident in his eyes. "Damn... I've been earning for years, and I have almost nothing to show for it."

"That's because you were stuck in the cycle of earning and spending without investing," Arjun said gently.

Sumant looked down at the table, ashamed. "I always thought I needed a higher salary to get ahead. I never considered making my money work for me."

Arjun placed a reassuring hand on his friend's shoulder. "It's not too late, Sumant. You can start now. It's about shifting your mindset. **Earn, invest, grow—then let your investments take care of you.**"

Sumant took a deep breath and nodded. "You're right. I can't keep living paycheck to paycheck. I need to change my financial habits."

A determined look crossed his face. For the first time in years, he felt like there was a way out of his financial struggles.

He wasn't just working to survive anymore.

He was ready to build wealth.

Achieving Financial Independence

A few months had passed since Arjun had introduced Sumant to the concept of passive income. While Sumant was still in the early stages of his financial transformation, Arjun himself had been making remarkable progress. Every month, his portfolio grew stronger, his dividends became larger, and his sense of security deepened.

One evening, as Arjun sat on his balcony, watching the sunset with a cup of chai, Eshwar arrived, as he often did, with a knowing smile on his face.

"You seem lost in thought," Eshwar said, taking a seat beside him.

Arjun chuckled. "Just reflecting on how far I've come. A year ago, I was stressed about my salary, about making ends meet. Now, my money is growing even when I'm not actively working for it."

Eshwar nodded. "That's the beauty of passive income. But tell me, Arjun—do you know when you'll be truly free?"

Arjun tilted his head. "What do you mean?"

Eshwar took a deep breath. "True financial independence is not just about having investments. It's about one simple equation: **When your passive income covers your living expenses, you no longer need to work for money.** That is when you are truly free."

Arjun sat up straighter, the weight of Eshwar's words sinking in. "So if my monthly expenses are ₹1,00,000, I need at least that much in passive income?"

"Exactly," Eshwar said. "Once your investments generate that amount every month, you will have the choice—the choice to work if you want to, not because you have to."

Arjun quickly grabbed a notepad and did the math. He calculated his current passive income from dividends, index funds, and rental properties. He was halfway there.

" ₹50,000 per month," Arjun murmured. "I've reached half of my target."

Eshwar smiled. "That's an incredible milestone. Most people don't even get that far because they never start. But you've built the foundation. Now, your job is simple—keep investing, keep growing, and in a few years, you'll reach complete financial independence."

Arjun felt a surge of determination. He was closer than he had ever imagined. The thought of not being tied to a job, of waking up every day without financial stress, was exhilarating.

"But what do I do once I get there?" Arjun asked, his voice tinged with curiosity.

Eshwar chuckled. "That, my friend, is the best part. Once you achieve financial independence, you get to **design your life on your own terms.** Travel, start a business, teach others, or simply spend time with your loved ones. You're no longer working for money—your money is working for you."

Arjun let out a slow breath. He could see it now—a future where he wasn't chained to a paycheck, where he had the freedom to live life on his own terms.

As the night grew darker, he looked up at the stars, a deep sense of peace settling within him.

He wasn't just building wealth anymore.

He was building freedom.

Key Takeaways from Chapter 9:

1. The Key to True Freedom

- Financial security is achieved when your money works for you, not the other way around.
- Passive income is the foundation of long-term financial independence.

2. Difference Between Active & Passive Income

- **Active Income** requires continuous work (salary, business profits).
- **Passive Income** keeps flowing even when you're not actively working (dividends, rental income, etc.).
- The goal is to replace active income with passive income over time.

3. The Power of Dividends

- Dividend-paying stocks provide regular income without selling investments.
- Reinvesting dividends accelerates wealth growth.

4. Real Estate as an Income Source

- Rental properties can generate steady monthly income.
- Using loans wisely can help build long-term real estate wealth.
- REITs (Real Estate Investment Trusts) allow investors to earn rental income without directly owning property.

5. **Digital Income Streams**

   - Online investments like index funds, ETFs, and REITs provide easy access to passive income.
   - Creating digital products (books, courses) can generate long-term earnings with minimal effort.

6. **Sumant's Wake-Up Call**

   - Relying only on a salary is risky; multiple income sources provide financial stability.
   - A shift from spending without saving to strategic investing is necessary for wealth building.

7. **Achieving Financial Independence**

   - Financial independence is reached when passive income covers all living expenses.
   - The equation: **Passive Income ≥ Monthly Expenses = Financial Freedom**
   - Once achieved, you have the freedom to work on your own terms, travel, or pursue passions without financial stress.

This chapter highlights the roadmap to building wealth beyond traditional employment, emphasizing long-term financial security.

CHAPTER TEN

The Right Asset Allocation

Why Asset Allocation Matters

Arjun sat at his desk, scrolling through his investment portfolio on his laptop. A mixture of emotions ran through his mind—satisfaction, curiosity, and a tinge of concern. Over the past few months, he had witnessed his stocks rise and fall. Some investments had delivered impressive gains, while others had declined unexpectedly.

"Why is this happening?" he muttered to himself. "Some stocks are booming, while others are sinking. How do I make sure my portfolio remains stable and grows consistently?"

The question nagged at him. He had read numerous investment articles, watched finance videos, and even discussed strategies with fellow investors. But no matter how much research he did, uncertainty lingered. He realized he had been picking stocks based on individual merits but hadn't considered how they all worked together.

Determined to find clarity, he reached out to Eshwar. That evening, they met at Eshwar's house, where the mentor welcomed him with his usual warm smile. Arjun wasted no time and got straight to the point.

"Eshwar, I've been investing for a while now, and I feel like I understand how to analyze stocks. But when I look at my portfolio, it feels... unbalanced. Some of my investments are doing great, while others are dragging me down. I want stability, but I also want growth. How do I achieve both?"

Eshwar chuckled knowingly. "Ah, Arjun, you've taken your first step toward truly mastering wealth creation. Stock selection is just one part of the game. The real magic happens when you learn asset allocation—how you balance your investments across different asset classes. This is what protects you from risk and ensures consistent growth."

He paused for a moment, then leaned forward. "Tell me, what would happen if you planted only mango trees in your garden?"

Arjun frowned. "Well... I'd have lots of mangoes."

"Yes, but what if there's a drought or a pest infestation that targets mango trees? You'd lose everything. But if you had a mix of mango trees, coconut trees, and vegetable plants, you'd still have something to rely on, even if one crop failed."

Arjun nodded slowly as the analogy sank in.

"The same applies to investments," Eshwar continued. "If you put all your money into one type of asset—whether it's stocks, real estate, or gold—you're taking a big risk. But if you distribute your wealth wisely, you can ensure growth while minimizing losses."

Arjun's eyes lit up with understanding. "So, I need to spread my investments across different asset classes?"

"Exactly! And not just randomly. You must allocate assets based on your goals, risk tolerance, and financial situation. Let me show you how."

Understanding Asset Classes

Eshwar stood up and walked to his bookshelf, pulling out an old notebook filled with scribbled notes and charts. He placed it in front of Arjun and flipped through the pages until he found what he was looking for.

"Investments are like tools in a toolbox. Each tool has a purpose, and if you use the wrong one for the job, you might end up making a mess instead of fixing the problem," he said. "Similarly, different asset classes serve different financial purposes. You need to understand them before deciding how to allocate your money."

Arjun leaned in eagerly as Eshwar began explaining.

1. Equities (Stocks) – The Engine of Growth

"Equities, or stocks, are the best way to grow wealth over the long term," Eshwar said, pointing to a line chart that showed the historical growth of the stock market. "Companies expand, economies grow, and when you own shares in successful businesses, your wealth grows along with them."

Arjun nodded. "I've seen how stocks can give massive returns over time. But they can also be risky, right?"

"Yes," Eshwar agreed. "Stocks are volatile. They fluctuate based on market sentiment, economic conditions, and company performance. That's why they're ideal for long-term investing. If you're patient and invest in strong businesses, equities can multiply your money over decades."

2. Fixed Income (Bonds, Fixed Deposits) – Stability & Security

Eshwar turned to another section of his notebook. "Now, let's talk about fixed-income investments—bonds, fixed deposits (FDs), and debt funds. These provide stability and steady returns."

"But aren't FDs and bonds low-return investments?" Arjun asked.

"True, but they serve a crucial purpose," Eshwar replied. "Not every part of your portfolio should be about chasing high returns. Fixed-income instruments ensure that even during market downturns, you have a source of steady income."

He pointed at a graph showing how bonds performed during market crashes. "When stock markets fall, investors move their money to safer assets like bonds, causing their value to rise. This creates a balance in your portfolio."

Arjun was beginning to see the bigger picture. "So, while stocks are for growth, fixed income is for stability?"

"Exactly," Eshwar said. "You need both to create a balanced investment plan."

3. Real Estate – A Tangible Asset with Long-Term Benefits

Arjun's eyes sparkled with interest as Eshwar moved to the next asset class—real estate. "I've always heard that real estate is a great investment. Is it really that good?"

Eshwar smiled. "Real estate has been a wealth-building tool for centuries. Owning land or property is like having a financial safety net. The value appreciates over time, and if you rent it out, you get a steady passive income."

He continued, "However, real estate isn't as liquid as stocks. You can't sell a house as easily as you sell shares. It also requires large capital and maintenance costs. That's why it should be a part of your portfolio, but not the entire portfolio."

Arjun was deep in thought. "I see. So real estate is great, but it shouldn't be my only focus."

"Correct," Eshwar said. "It's one of the many tools in your financial toolbox."

4. Gold & Commodities – The Shield Against Inflation

Eshwar then moved to the next category. "Gold and commodities act as a hedge against inflation and financial crises."

"How?" Arjun asked, intrigued.

"Because gold holds its value when currencies lose theirs. Think about it—during uncertain times, people rush to buy gold, pushing its price up. It's not meant for high returns like stocks, but it's great for preserving wealth."

Arjun thought back to stories of his grandmother buying gold jewelry as an investment. "So, it's a defensive asset?"

"Exactly. A small portion of your portfolio in gold can protect you during uncertain times."

5. Cash & Liquid Funds – The Emergency Buffer

Finally, Eshwar pointed to the last category. "Cash and liquid funds are crucial. They are your emergency cushion."

"But shouldn't all money be invested?" Arjun questioned.

"Not all of it," Eshwar said firmly. "You should always have an emergency fund that can cover at least 6 to 12 months of expenses. This ensures that if something unexpected happens—a job loss, medical emergency, or market crash—you won't have to sell your investments at a loss."

Arjun nodded. "That makes sense. Having cash reserves prevents me from making panic decisions."

"Exactly," Eshwar smiled. "Asset allocation isn't about chasing returns—it's about building a strategy that allows you to sleep peacefully at night, knowing your money is working for you while being protected from risks."

Arjun took a deep breath, absorbing all the new knowledge. "I never realized how important asset allocation was. I thought investing was just about picking good stocks."

Eshwar chuckled. "Most people make that mistake. But now you know better. Next, let's discuss how to allocate assets based on your specific financial situation."

The 3 Golden Rules of Asset Allocation

Eshwar leaned back in his chair, stretching his arms. "Now that you understand different asset classes, let's talk about how to distribute your money among them. This is where most investors go wrong."

Arjun was eager to learn more. "How do I decide how much to allocate to each asset?"

Eshwar smiled. "There's no one-size-fits-all formula, but there are three golden rules that guide asset allocation. Follow these, and you'll build a strong, resilient portfolio."

Rule #1: Diversification is Key

"Diversification simply means not putting all your eggs in one basket," Eshwar explained. "Imagine if you invested everything in one stock, and that company went bankrupt. You'd lose everything."

Arjun nodded. "That makes sense. But how much should I diversify?"

"Enough to reduce risk, but not so much that it becomes unmanageable," Eshwar said. "For example, if you invest in ten stocks across different sectors, you're diversified. But if you own 100 stocks, managing them becomes difficult, and the returns may not be much better than an index fund."

Arjun thought for a moment. "So, a balance is needed. Enough diversification to lower risk but not so much that it dilutes returns."

"Exactly," Eshwar said. "And diversification isn't just about stocks. It's about spreading your investments across different asset classes—equities, fixed income, real estate, gold, and cash. This way, when one asset underperforms, others compensate for it."

Rule #2: Risk Tolerance Matters

"Every investor has a different risk tolerance," Eshwar continued. "A 25-year-old can afford to take more risks than a 60-year-old retiree."

Arjun nodded. "Because younger investors have more time to recover from losses?"

"Precisely. When you're young, you can invest more in stocks because you have years ahead to ride out market volatility. But as you approach retirement, you should shift more towards stable assets like bonds and fixed deposits to preserve wealth."

Eshwar handed Arjun a simple guideline:

- **Aggressive Investors (Young, High Risk Tolerance)** → 70-80% Stocks, 10-20% Bonds, 5-10% Others
- **Moderate Investors (Balanced Approach)** → 50-60% Stocks, 30-40% Bonds, 10% Others
- **Conservative Investors (Near Retirement, Low Risk Tolerance)** → 30-40% Stocks, 50-60% Bonds, 10% Others

Arjun studied the table carefully. "So, my allocation should depend on my age and financial goals?"

"Exactly," Eshwar said. "And it should evolve as you grow older and your risk tolerance changes."

Rule #3: Rebalancing is Necessary

"Asset allocation is not something you set once and forget," Eshwar warned. "You must rebalance your portfolio regularly."

"What does rebalancing mean?" Arjun asked.

"It means adjusting your investments periodically to maintain the right balance," Eshwar explained. "For example, suppose you initially allocated 60% to stocks and 20% to bonds. After a year, stocks may have grown significantly, making up 75% of your portfolio. That means your portfolio has become riskier than you originally planned."

Arjun's eyes widened. "So I need to sell some stocks and buy bonds to restore balance?"

"Exactly!" Eshwar said. "That's rebalancing. It helps you stay aligned with your financial goals and risk tolerance."

Arjun was fascinated. "How often should I rebalance?"

"Every 6 to 12 months," Eshwar suggested. "Or whenever your asset allocation drifts too far from your target."

Arjun leaned back, processing everything. "This makes so much sense. I always thought investing was about picking the best stocks, but now I realize it's about maintaining the right balance."

Eshwar smiled. "You've learned one of the most important lessons in wealth creation. Master asset allocation, and you'll never have to worry about market fluctuations again."

Arjun's Personalized Portfolio Allocation

A few days later, Arjun sat down with Eshwar in their usual café, his mind brimming with thoughts. "Eshwar, I understand the rules of asset allocation now. But how do I apply them to my investments? How do I build a portfolio that works for me?"

Eshwar took a sip of his tea and smiled. "Good question, Arjun. Asset allocation isn't about copying someone else's portfolio. It's about designing one that suits your age, risk tolerance, and financial goals."

"Okay," Arjun said, pulling out his notepad. "Where do we start?"

Step 1: Understanding Goals and Time Horizon

"First," Eshwar began, "you need to define your financial goals. Are you investing for retirement, a house, or financial independence?"

Arjun thought for a moment. "I want financial freedom as soon as possible. I don't want to work until retirement age."

"Good," Eshwar said. "That means you need a portfolio that focuses on both long-term growth and passive income."

Arjun nodded. "That makes sense. So, what's next?"

Step 2: Choosing the Right Allocation

Eshwar grabbed a pen and started sketching a simple allocation plan:

Arjun's Personalized Portfolio Allocation

60% in Equities – "Since you're young, most of your money should be in stocks. Stocks give high returns in the long run, but they can be volatile."

20% in Fixed Income – "This is for stability. You'll invest in government bonds, fixed deposits, or debt funds to create a safety net."

10% in Real Estate – "Real estate is good for long-term wealth, but it requires significant capital. We'll start small, maybe through REITs (Real Estate Investment Trusts)."

5% in Gold & Commodities – "Gold acts as an inflation hedge and protects against market crashes."

5% in Cash & Liquid Funds – "Emergency funds for unexpected expenses. This will ensure you don't have to sell stocks in bad market conditions."

Arjun studied the allocation. "This looks balanced. But why only 5% in cash? Shouldn't I keep more money in my savings account?"

Eshwar shook his head. "Keeping too much in savings is a mistake. Inflation eats away at your money. You should keep only what you need for emergencies."

Arjun was beginning to see the bigger picture. "I get it now. My money should be working for me, not sitting idle."

Step 3: Implementing the Plan

"Now that we have the allocation," Eshwar continued, "the next step is to invest consistently. You don't have to invest everything at once. Use a Systematic Investment Plan (SIP) for stocks and mutual funds."

"SIP?" Arjun asked.

"It's a way to invest small amounts regularly instead of putting all your money in at once. This helps you buy at different market levels and reduces risk."

Arjun was impressed. "That sounds perfect for me. I don't have a huge amount to invest upfront, but I can contribute monthly."

Eshwar smiled. "That's the right approach. Wealth is built over time, not overnight."

Arjun felt a new level of confidence. He was no longer just picking stocks randomly—he was building a strategy that could sustain him for life.

Sumant's Risky Investment Strategy

While Arjun was carefully planning his portfolio with Eshwar's guidance, Sumant was taking a completely different approach. He was still chasing quick money, believing that picking the right stocks would make him rich overnight.

One evening, Arjun met Sumant at a café after work. Sumant looked excited, his eyes shining with enthusiasm.

"Arjun, you won't believe it! I just found a stock that's been doubling every few months. If I put in a lakh today, I could make two lakhs in no time!"

Arjun raised an eyebrow. "Which stock is this?"

Sumant pulled out his phone and showed Arjun a chart of a small, unknown company. "Look at this! It shot up 300% in just six months. It's the next big thing, I tell you!"

Arjun sighed. "Sumant, have you researched this company? Do you know what it does, how profitable it is, or if it has strong fundamentals?"

Sumant waved a hand dismissively. "Who cares about all that? The stock is going up, and that's all that matters! I'm putting all my savings into it."

The Danger of Chasing Quick Gains

Over the next few weeks, Sumant kept investing in high-risk stocks, believing he had cracked the code to making money. Every day, he would check stock prices, celebrate small gains, and panic when prices dropped.

One day, the stock he had invested in—his "next big thing"—suddenly crashed by 50% in a single day. A news article revealed that the company was involved in financial fraud, and investors were dumping their shares.

Sumant's phone buzzed continuously with alerts—his portfolio was in the red. He frantically called Arjun.

"Arjun! My stocks are crashing! I've lost half my money in just one day! What should I do?"

Arjun remained calm. "Sumant, didn't I tell you that blindly chasing rising stocks is dangerous? You didn't diversify, and now all your money is tied up in one bad investment."

Sumant was silent for a moment, then groaned. "I thought I could make quick money. But now I don't know what to do."

Learning the Hard Way

Sumant sat with Arjun and Eshwar that evening, visibly shaken. "I thought the stock market was about picking the right stocks and getting rich fast. But I didn't realize how risky it was."

Eshwar nodded. "The market rewards those who are patient and disciplined. Wealth isn't built overnight—it's built with smart investing and proper asset allocation."

Sumant looked at Arjun. "So, what should I do now?"

Arjun smiled. "Start from scratch. Learn about asset allocation, invest wisely, and stop chasing quick money. If you're serious, we'll help you build a proper portfolio."

Sumant took a deep breath. "Okay. I've learned my lesson. No more gambling. I want to do this the right way."

For the first time, Sumant truly understood the importance of discipline in investing. He was ready to turn things around.

The Importance of Portfolio Rebalancing

With Sumant now willing to take a disciplined approach, Eshwar decided it was the perfect time to introduce one of the most critical yet often overlooked aspects of investing—**portfolio rebalancing**.

One evening, as Arjun and Sumant gathered at Eshwar's home, he placed two identical glasses of water in front of them.

"Imagine these glasses represent your investment portfolio," he said. Then, he took a spoonful of salt and added it to one of the glasses while leaving the other untouched.

"What do you think will happen if I keep adding more and more salt to just one glass?" Eshwar asked.

"It'll become too salty to drink," Arjun replied.

"Exactly!" Eshwar smiled. "Just like an unbalanced portfolio. If you let one asset grow too much while ignoring others, your portfolio becomes too risky. You need to adjust it from time to time to maintain balance—just like you would dilute the salty water to make it drinkable again."

Why Rebalancing Matters

Eshwar leaned back and explained, "When you first allocate your investments, everything is in proportion. But over time, some assets will grow faster than others. If you don't rebalance, you might end up with a portfolio that's completely different from what you originally planned."

He pulled up a real-life example. "Let's say you start with this allocation:

- 60% in equities
- 20% in fixed income
- 10% in real estate
- 5% in gold
- 5% in cash & liquid funds"

Arjun nodded, remembering that this was the portfolio allocation Eshwar had helped him set up.

"Now," Eshwar continued, "if the stock market has a great year, your equities might grow so much that they make up 75% of your portfolio, while fixed income and other assets shrink in proportion. If you don't rebalance, you'll be overexposed to stock market risks."

Arjun's eyes widened. "So, if a market crash happens, I could lose a big chunk of my wealth just because I didn't rebalance?"

"Exactly!" Eshwar confirmed. "Rebalancing means selling some of the overgrown assets and reinvesting in underperforming ones to bring your portfolio back to the original balance."

When and How to Rebalance

Sumant, now paying full attention, asked, "How often should we rebalance?"

Eshwar smiled. "Good question. There's no fixed rule, but most experienced investors check their portfolios **every 6 to 12 months**. Some do it when their asset allocation shifts beyond a certain percentage—say, if stocks go from 60% to 70%, they rebalance."

Arjun was now thinking ahead. "And when we rebalance, do we just sell stocks and buy bonds?"

"Not necessarily," Eshwar replied. "You can do it in different ways:

1. **By Selling & Buying** – Sell high-performing assets and buy the ones lagging behind.
2. **By Adjusting Future Investments** – Instead of selling, you direct new investments into underweighted assets. For example, if stocks have grown too much, you stop buying stocks for a while and invest in bonds or real estate instead."

Sumant shook his head. "I never even thought about all this. No wonder I kept losing money—I was just putting it wherever I thought I'd get quick returns."

Arjun smiled at him. "That was me before I met Eshwar. You're on the right path now."

Arjun's New Perspective

After understanding the importance of rebalancing, Arjun made it a habit to check his portfolio every six months. Instead of blindly chasing high returns, he now focused on maintaining balance.

One year later, during a market downturn, Arjun saw that while stocks were falling, his fixed-income investments and gold were stable. His portfolio took a hit, but much less than it would have if he had been fully invested in equities.

Meanwhile, Sumant, who had started applying the principles he learned, had begun seeing positive changes in his own financial situation. Though he was still learning, he was no longer gambling—he was investing.

The Chapter's Final Lesson

As Arjun sat with Eshwar one evening, he reflected on how much he had grown.

"Asset allocation isn't just about investing," he said thoughtfully. "It's about managing risk, making sure I don't put everything in one basket, and keeping my emotions in check."

Eshwar nodded. "The goal isn't just to make money. It's to keep it, grow it, and protect it. Smart investing is about discipline, patience, and consistency. And now, you're on your way to mastering it."

Arjun smiled, feeling more confident than ever. He knew that financial success wasn't about luck—it was about making **the right choices, at the right time, with the right mindset**.

With that, the lesson of **The Right Asset Allocation** was complete, and Arjun was now prepared for the next step in his journey toward **financial independence**.

CHAPTER ELEVEN

The art of Budgeting

1. The Wake-Up Call: Where Does the Money Go?

It was a warm Saturday evening. Arjun had just finished reviewing his investment portfolio. His stock holdings were performing well, his mutual funds were compounding steadily, and he even had a decent emergency fund in place. By all measures, he was **on the right track financially.**

Yet, something was bothering him. **Why was his bank balance not growing as much as he expected?**

Each month, his salary got credited. Each month, he saved a portion of it. And yet, by the time the next salary arrived, his savings felt disappointingly small. **Where was all the money going?**

For months, Arjun had ignored this thought, assuming it was normal. But today, that nagging feeling refused to go away.

Just then, **Suneetha walked into the room**, holding a few shopping bags. She placed them on the table and sighed, looking exhausted.

"Shopping again?" Arjun asked playfully.

"Not for me," Suneetha said. *"It's just groceries and a few household things."*

She slumped onto the sofa and looked at Arjun, a little hesitant.

"Arjun... can we talk about something?" she asked.

Arjun immediately sensed the seriousness in her tone. He put his phone down and turned toward her.

"What happened?" he asked.

Suneetha hesitated for a moment before speaking.

"I've been noticing something for a while now. We're earning well, you've built a solid investment portfolio, and yet... at the end of the month, there's barely anything left. Doesn't that seem strange to you?"

Arjun frowned. *"What do you mean? I've been saving and investing regularly. Expenses are just a part of life."*

Suneetha shook her head.

"I'm not talking about basic expenses. I mean, really think about it, Arjun. Every month, we plan to save more, but somehow, by the end of the month, we barely have anything extra. I don't even know where all the money is going!"

Her words hit Arjun like a **bolt of lightning.**

He had **felt the same thing** but had never truly confronted it. Instead, he had convinced himself that as long as he was investing, things were fine.

But now, hearing Suneetha voice the exact thought that had been bothering him, **he couldn't ignore it anymore.**

"You think we're overspending?" he asked, his curiosity piqued.

"I don't know," Suneetha admitted. *"But I do know this—no matter how much we earn, if we don't keep track of where it goes, we'll never feel financially secure."*

Arjun leaned back, absorbing her words.

Had he been so focused on investing that he had neglected the most basic financial principle—spending control?

For years, he had assumed that as long as he was putting money into the stock market, he was making progress. But what if his **unconscious spending habits** were **silently draining his wealth?**

His mind drifted back to a conversation he had with **Eshwar** months ago—the very first lesson about tracking expenses. Back then, it had seemed simple.

"Reduce unnecessary spending and invest the difference," Eshwar had told him.

Arjun had followed the investing part religiously. But what about the **expense-tracking part?** Had he truly been mindful of where his money was going?

A sudden **realization dawned upon him.**

"Suneetha, we need to fix this," he said with determination.

"I agree," she nodded.

"I think I need to talk to Eshwar again. I need to understand where we're going wrong," Arjun said.

Suneetha smiled. *"You always go to Eshwar when you need financial wisdom, don't you?"*

Arjun laughed. *"Well, I don't want to repeat the same mistakes I made in the past. If we want to build real wealth, we can't just rely on earning more—we have to manage what we have."*

That night, **Arjun made a firm decision.**

He wasn't going to let his hard-earned money slip away unnoticed. He was going to **get to the bottom of this mystery.**

First thing in the morning, he would meet Eshwar and **learn the true art of budgeting.**

2. Why Budgeting is Essential for Wealth Building

The next morning, Arjun walked into the familiar café where he often met Eshwar. He ordered two cups of filter coffee—one for himself and one for his mentor.

As he waited, he pulled out his phone and opened his banking app. He scrolled through the transactions of the past month, his eyes darting over numerous small but frequent expenses— ₹199 for an OTT subscription, ₹599 for a premium food delivery service, ₹2,300 for a "flash sale" on a shopping app, and countless ₹200- ₹300 transactions from cafes and restaurants.

It all seemed harmless individually. But when added up, the total was shocking.

"No wonder my savings aren't growing," he muttered under his breath.

Just then, Eshwar walked in, his calm presence bringing a sense of reassurance.

"Good morning, Arjun! You look like a man deep in thought," Eshwar said, taking his seat.

Arjun sighed. *"Eshwar, I need your advice again. I've been investing regularly, but at the end of each month, I feel like my money just... disappears. No matter how much I earn, I don't seem to have much left. I thought I was doing everything right, but now I feel like I'm missing something."*

Eshwar smiled knowingly. *"Ah, so you've reached the next stage of financial awareness. That's good. Tell me, have you been tracking your spending?"*

Arjun hesitated. *"Not really. I mean, I know my big expenses—EMIs, rent, investments—but I never bothered tracking the small stuff. Does it really make that much of a difference?"*

Eshwar leaned back and took a sip of his coffee.

"Arjun, let me tell you a secret that many people, even high-income earners, don't realize. It's not just about how much you earn. It's about how much you keep. If you don't control your money, your money will control you."

Arjun frowned. *"What do you mean?"*

Eshwar placed his cup down and folded his arms.

"Many people assume that budgeting is only for those who struggle financially. But do you know that even the world's richest people follow a strict budget? It's because budgeting isn't about restricting yourself—it's about directing your money towards things that truly matter."

Arjun was intrigued. *"But I'm already investing. Isn't that enough?"*

Eshwar shook his head. *"Investing is only half the equation. Think of it this way—if you earn ₹1,00,000 per month but unknowingly spend ₹90,000, what are you left with?"*

" ₹10,000," Arjun said.

"Now imagine if you were earning just ₹50,000 but had complete control over your spending, saving ₹15,000 every month. Who is in a better financial position?"

Arjun thought for a moment. *"The second person... because they're actually saving more."*

Eshwar nodded. *"Exactly. Your income means nothing if you don't manage it properly. That's why budgeting is essential—not just for saving money, but for achieving financial freedom faster."*

Arjun's eyes widened as realization dawned upon him.

"I never thought of it that way. I always assumed that if I kept earning more, my wealth would grow automatically. But if I'm not managing it well, I could be earning crores and still feel financially stuck."

"Precisely," Eshwar said. *"Budgeting helps you in three key ways:"*

1. Control Spending – Avoid Unnecessary Expenses

"When you don't have a budget, your spending is dictated by impulses. You buy things because they seem affordable at

the moment. But when you add them up, they silently eat away at your financial growth. A budget gives you control over where your money goes."

Arjun thought about the unnecessary online shopping he had done in the past few months. He had never realized how much these small expenses had accumulated.

2. Prioritize Goals – Align Money with Future Aspirations

"Do you know what separates the wealthy from the financially stuck?" Eshwar asked.

"Discipline?" Arjun guessed.

"Not just that. The wealthy always align their spending with their goals. Every rupee they spend has a purpose. Do you have clear financial goals?"

Arjun nodded slowly. *"Yes. I want to achieve financial independence and retire early."*

"Then every rupee you spend should bring you closer to that goal, not take you further away. A budget ensures that your money is working for you, not against you."

3. Achieve Financial Independence – Ensure Every Rupee Has a Role

"Many people assume financial independence is only about making money. But real financial independence is about knowing that your money is being used in the best possible way. When you budget properly, you're not just saving—you're accelerating your journey to wealth."

Arjun leaned back, deep in thought.

"I see it now," he said. *"Budgeting isn't about restricting myself—it's about giving my money a direction. Without a budget, I'm just letting my income flow away aimlessly."*

Eshwar smiled. *"Now you're thinking like a true wealth builder."*

Arjun took a deep breath. He had always seen budgeting as something boring, something meant for people who struggled with money. But now, he realized that **budgeting was the very foundation of financial success.**

Beyond Basic Budgeting: Financial Optimization

Arjun had been following the **50-30-20 rule** for several months now, and while he had successfully cut down unnecessary expenses, he couldn't shake off a nagging feeling.

One evening, as he sat down to review his finances, he noticed something strange—**even though he was saving 20% of his income, his wealth wasn't growing as fast as he had expected.** The balance in his savings account had increased, but it wasn't generating significant returns.

Eshwar Introduces the Concept of Financial Optimization

"So, tell me, what's on your mind?" Eshwar asked.

Arjun leaned forward. "I've been following the budgeting rule diligently. I've controlled my spending, saved 20% of my income, and even tracked my expenses. But despite all that, my savings aren't growing the way I expected. What am I missing?"

Eshwar smiled knowingly. "Ah, you've reached an important milestone, Arjun. **Budgeting is just the first step. The next step is making sure your savings work for you.** It's time you move from just saving to **financial optimization.**"

Arjun raised an eyebrow. "Financial optimization?"

"Yes," Eshwar said, taking a sip of his tea. "It's not just about how much you save—it's about **where your money is going and whether it's being put to work.** Right now, if most of your savings are sitting idle in a low-interest savings account, you're losing money to inflation."

Arjun frowned. "So what should I do?"

1. Segmenting Savings for Maximum Growth

Eshwar pulled out a piece of paper and drew three circles.

"Think of your savings as three different buckets," he explained. "Each bucket serves a different purpose, and you must allocate money accordingly."

Bucket 1: Emergency Fund (6 Months of Expenses)

"This is the money you must keep liquid—meaning, it should be accessible at any time. Ideally, this should be kept in a high-yield savings account, a fixed deposit, or a liquid mutual fund."

Arjun nodded. "That makes sense. I already have some money set aside for emergencies, but I never really thought about how to park it efficiently."

Bucket 2: Short-Term Goals (1-3 Years)

"These are funds for any planned expenses coming up soon—buying a car, a vacation, a down payment for a house, or even further education. You should park this in safer options like debt mutual funds or recurring deposits, where they grow steadily but are not at risk."

Arjun started taking notes. "So, I shouldn't put all my money in a single place but rather categorize it based on when I need it?"

"Exactly," Eshwar said.

Bucket 3: Long-Term Wealth Building (5+ Years)

"Now, this is the most important bucket. This is the money that will make you financially free. Instead of just keeping it in savings, you must invest it—**in stocks, mutual funds, real estate, and other assets that generate higher returns.**"

Arjun's eyes widened. "So, I've been keeping all my money in one place when I should have been directing it towards different purposes!"

Eshwar smiled. "Now you're getting it."

2. Identifying & Eliminating Invisible Expenses

Arjun felt a sense of clarity, but something still puzzled him.

"I've cut down on unnecessary expenses like eating out and impulsive shopping, but I still feel like I could save more. What else am I missing?"

Eshwar leaned back and said, "There's something called **invisible expenses.** These are expenses that don't seem significant individually, but they quietly drain your money."

Arjun's curiosity grew. "Like what?"

Eshwar listed a few:

- **Subscription traps** – Many people sign up for online services (OTT platforms, premium apps, gym memberships) and forget about them, even if they rarely use them.
- **High-interest EMIs & credit card payments** – Paying the minimum due on a credit card leads to massive interest charges.
- **Excess insurance** – Many people pay for policies they don't need.
- **Online impulse buys** – Flash sales and discounts create an illusion of savings but encourage unnecessary spending.

Arjun pulled out his phone and checked his recent transactions. He was shocked. He still had an old gym membership active that he hadn't used in months, along with three different OTT platform subscriptions he barely watched.

"Wow... I didn't even realize I was spending on these," he muttered.

"That's why I call them **invisible expenses**," Eshwar said with a chuckle.

Arjun immediately made a plan to **cancel unused subscriptions, shift high-interest EMIs to lower-interest loans, and optimize his insurance.**

3. Cash Flow Automation: Making Money Flow Effortlessly

Eshwar then introduced Arjun to an even more powerful concept.

"Now that you know how to allocate money efficiently, let me show you a trick that makes budgeting effortless."

Arjun was all ears.

"It's called **cash flow automation.**"

Eshwar explained:

- Instead of manually transferring money into different accounts, **automate everything.**
- The moment salary is credited, an **auto-transfer sends a fixed percentage to savings and investments.**
- Monthly bills and necessary expenses are deducted automatically.
- This way, Arjun **only sees the money he is allowed to spend.**

Arjun's eyes lit up. "This means I won't have to rely on willpower to save! The money will be saved before I even get a chance to spend it."

Eshwar smiled. "Yes, and that's how the wealthy stay disciplined with their money."

Arjun immediately set up standing instructions on his bank account—**40% of his salary would be auto-invested** before he could even touch it.

Arjun's Realization: Budgeting is Not Restrictive, It's Empowering

A few months later, Arjun noticed a drastic change in his finances:

- His **savings had grown significantly** since he had directed them into the right investment buckets.
- By cutting down invisible expenses, he had **more surplus money than before.**
- Thanks to **automation, saving had become effortless,** and he didn't have to manually allocate money every month.

One evening, he shared his success with Suneetha.

She smiled, "You know, earlier I used to think budgeting meant restricting ourselves. But now, I see it's actually making our life better. We don't feel deprived, and we're more in control than ever before."

Arjun nodded. "Exactly! Budgeting is not about limiting ourselves—it's about **giving every rupee a purpose.**"

Suneetha hugged him. "I'm proud of us."

Arjun smiled. For the first time, he felt not just financially stable, but financially **empowered.**

CHAPTER TWELVE

The Role of Insurance in Financial Planning

1. The Unexpected Crisis

One evening, Arjun was going through his emails when he noticed a message in his office group. A colleague, Rajesh, had suddenly passed away due to a heart attack, leaving behind his wife and two young children. The group was actively collecting donations to support his grieving family.

Arjun felt a pang of sorrow. He had met Rajesh only a few times but knew he was a responsible family man. The tragedy weighed on him. Later that night, as he lay in bed, he turned to Suneetha and said, "Did you hear about Rajesh? His wife now has to manage everything on her own."

Suneetha nodded, equally disturbed. "Yes, and she's a homemaker. Without Rajesh's income, how will they manage the expenses? Their kids are still in school."

This conversation lingered in Arjun's mind. The next day, he met Eshwar and shared his concerns. "I can't stop thinking about Rajesh's family. I'm wondering—what would happen if something like that happened to me?"

Eshwar listened carefully and then asked, "Tell me, Arjun, if you weren't around tomorrow, would Suneetha and your child be financially secure?"

The question hit Arjun hard. He had been so focused on investments, savings, and expenses that he had never thought about this aspect of financial planning. "I have some savings, but I don't think it would last them for long. Plus, I don't have a dedicated plan for such a situation."

Eshwar leaned back and said, "This is exactly why we need insurance. It's not about you—it's about your family's future."

2. Understanding the Core Purpose of Insurance

Arjun always viewed insurance as just another financial product—something agents push for commissions. But Eshwar made him see it differently.

"Insurance is not an investment," Eshwar began. "It is a risk management tool. It exists for one reason: to protect your family from financial distress in your absence or during a crisis."

He broke insurance down into three essential categories:

1. **Life Insurance** – Provides financial security to the family if the primary earner is no longer around.
2. **Health Insurance** – Covers medical emergencies and rising healthcare costs.
3. **General Insurance** – Protects assets like home, vehicle, and business.

Arjun recalled that his company provided health insurance, but he never really checked the coverage details. He also had a life insurance policy, but it was an endowment plan suggested by a distant relative. He never questioned whether it was enough.

"This means if something happens to me," Arjun said, "Suneetha will have to rely on our savings and investments. But if those are not sufficient, she might face financial difficulties."

"Exactly," Eshwar said. "The purpose of insurance is to ensure that financial troubles don't compound emotional distress."

3. Life Insurance: Ensuring Family's Financial Security

Arjun sat across from Eshwar, still processing their discussion. "I do have a life insurance policy," he said hesitantly. "I took it a few years ago because my relative insisted. But to be honest, I never really checked whether it's actually useful."

Eshwar smiled knowingly. "Let me guess—it's an endowment plan or a ULIP?"

Arjun nodded. "Yes, it offers life coverage, but it also promises a maturity amount after 20 years."

"That's the problem with most traditional plans," Eshwar explained. "They mix investment with insurance and end up doing neither well."

He picked up a notepad and started drawing a simple table.

Two Primary Types of Life Insurance:

1. **Term Insurance** – A pure life cover that pays a lump sum to the family in case of the policyholder's death.
2. **Traditional Plans (Endowment, ULIPs, etc.)** – Mixes insurance with savings or investments, offering lower coverage at higher premiums.

Eshwar circled "Term Insurance" and continued, "This is what you actually need. It gives your family the highest financial protection for the lowest cost."

Arjun frowned. "But isn't it better to take a policy that gives returns?"

"That's the mistake most people make," Eshwar said. "Let me ask you this—if something happens to you, would you want your family to receive ₹1 crore or just ₹10 lakh?"

"Obviously ₹1 crore," Arjun said without hesitation.

"Then term insurance is your answer. Endowment plans offer a smaller sum assured because they divert your premium into investments. That's why the coverage is so low. But with term insurance, you can get ₹1 crore coverage at a fraction of the cost."

Arjun was starting to understand. "So how much coverage should I have?"

"As a general rule, at least **10 to 15 times your annual income**," Eshwar advised. "This ensures that your family has enough financial support in your absence."

Arjun did a quick mental calculation. His current annual income was ₹12 lakh. "That means I should have at least ₹1.2 crore in life coverage," he murmured.

Eshwar nodded. "Exactly. And you need to ensure that Suneetha is the nominee so that the funds reach her directly."

That evening, Arjun reviewed his existing insurance policies. His endowment plan barely covered ₹10 lakh—far below what was needed. The realization hit him hard. His family was financially vulnerable.

The next day, he applied for a term insurance policy with a ₹1.5 crore sum assured. For the first time, he felt a sense of relief. He was securing his family's future, not just investing for returns.

4. Health Insurance: Protecting Against Medical Expenses

A few weeks after taking his term insurance policy, Arjun was visiting a colleague in the hospital. The colleague's father had suffered a heart attack and was undergoing treatment. While talking to him, Arjun learned that the medical bills had already crossed ₹8 lakh in just a few days.

"I had to break my fixed deposits," his colleague sighed. "I never thought we'd need this much money so soon."

Arjun felt a pang of concern. What if something like this happened in his family? Would he have enough savings to handle it? He had some health insurance from his employer, but he had never really checked the details.

Later that evening, he brought up the topic with Eshwar. "I have health insurance from my company, but I'm not sure if it's enough," he admitted.

Eshwar leaned back and asked, "How much is the coverage?"

Arjun checked his phone and replied, "₹3 lakh for me, and another ₹3 lakh as a floater for my family."

Eshwar shook his head. "That's not enough. Medical costs are skyrocketing. A single major surgery could wipe out that entire coverage."

"So, what should I do?" Arjun asked, feeling uneasy.

Eshwar picked up his notepad and listed down the main types of health insurance:

1. **Individual Health Plan** – Covers a single person, best for those without dependents.
2. **Family Floater Plan** – Covers the entire family under one policy, making it more cost-effective.

3. **Critical Illness Plan** – Pays a lump sum if diagnosed with diseases like cancer or heart attack.
4. **Top-up Plans** – Helps extend coverage beyond the base policy, useful when employer insurance is insufficient.

Arjun's eyes scanned the list. "So, should I get a Family Floater Plan?"

"Yes," Eshwar said. "You should have at least ₹10–25 lakh coverage for your family, depending on your city and lifestyle."

"But won't that be expensive?" Arjun hesitated.

"Not as expensive as a medical emergency," Eshwar said firmly. "Plus, if you buy early, premiums are lower. Think of it as a small price for peace of mind."

Arjun understood. He didn't want to be in a situation where he had to scramble for money during a crisis. That night, he researched different health insurance providers and finalized a family floater plan with ₹15 lakh coverage.

As he clicked the payment button, he felt something shift inside him. For the first time, he was truly preparing for his family's future, not just reacting to problems as they came.

5. Disability and Accident Insurance: Preparing for Unforeseen Events

A month after securing his health insurance, Arjun was driving home from work when he saw a terrible accident on the highway. A bike lay mangled on the road, and a man was being lifted onto a stretcher. His mind flashed to Vasu Dev, his college friend who had met with a similar accident a few years ago.

Back then, Vasu Dev had been the sole breadwinner of his family. The accident left him with a permanent spinal injury, forcing him to quit his job. With no income and rising medical expenses, his family had gone through a financial nightmare. Arjun still remembered visiting Vasu Dev in the hospital, seeing the helplessness in his eyes.

That evening, as he sat with Eshwar, the memory of Vasu Dev's struggle weighed heavily on his mind. "Eshwar, I never really thought about it before, but what if I get into an accident and can't work anymore?"

Eshwar nodded, as if he had been waiting for this question. "That's exactly why you need **Personal Accident Insurance and Disability Insurance**."

Arjun leaned forward. "I already have life and health insurance. Isn't that enough?"

Eshwar smiled. "Life insurance takes care of your family if you're gone. Health insurance covers hospital bills. But what if you survive an accident and can't work anymore? How will you manage daily expenses?"

That question hit Arjun hard. He had always assumed insurance was for death or medical emergencies, but he had never considered the possibility of long-term disability.

Eshwar continued, listing the two key types of coverage:

1. **Personal Accident Insurance** – Provides a lump sum payout in case of accidental death or permanent disability.
2. **Disability Insurance** – Ensures a steady monthly income if an accident or illness prevents you from working.

Arjun listened carefully. "So, Personal Accident Insurance gives a lump sum, and Disability Insurance gives a regular income?"

"Exactly," Eshwar confirmed. "Personal Accident Insurance helps your family recover financially if something happens to you. But Disability Insurance ensures you still have an income if you survive but can't work."

Arjun's mind raced. "How much coverage should I get?"

"For Personal Accident Insurance, at least **10 times your annual income**," Eshwar advised. "For Disability Insurance, try to get a plan that replaces **at least 50–60% of your current income**."

Arjun exhaled. "I never even thought about this before. I've insured my car, but I never insured myself against accidents."

Eshwar chuckled. "That's the irony. People insure their vehicles but forget to insure their own income. Remember, your ability to earn is your biggest asset."

The next day, Arjun did his research and signed up for both Personal Accident and Disability Insurance. As he completed the process, he felt a deep sense of relief. He had seen what happened to families caught unprepared. Now, no matter what life threw at him, he knew his family would be financially secure.

6. Protecting Assets: Home, Car, and Business Insurance

One evening, as Arjun scrolled through his phone, a news article caught his attention. A well-known residential apartment complex in his city had caught fire, leaving dozens of families homeless. The report mentioned that many residents had lost everything—furniture, appliances, jewelry, important documents—and only a handful had insurance to recover their losses.

Arjun's heart sank. He imagined what would happen if a disaster struck his own home. He and Suneetha had worked hard to make their house a comfortable place for their family. Losing it all overnight would be devastating.

That night, over dinner, he brought up the topic with Suneetha. "Do we have home insurance?"

Suneetha frowned. "I don't think so. But why? What happened?"

Arjun explained about the fire accident. "I always thought home insurance was unnecessary. But now I realize that if something like that happened to us, we'd have to start from scratch."

Seeing his concern, she nodded. "We should look into it."

The next day, Arjun met with Eshwar and brought up the topic.

Eshwar smiled. "You're thinking ahead, Arjun. Most people assume nothing bad will ever happen to them—until it does."

"I never thought about insuring my house," Arjun admitted. "Can you tell me how it works?"

Eshwar explained, "Home insurance covers losses due to fire, theft, natural disasters, and even structural damage. There are two main types of coverage:

1. **Building Insurance** – Covers the structure of the house, including walls, roofs, and floors.
2. **Contents Insurance** – Covers household items like furniture, electronics, and valuables."

Arjun was surprised. "So, even if an earthquake or fire damages my house, I won't have to bear the full loss?"

"Exactly," Eshwar confirmed. "And if your belongings are stolen or destroyed, the insurance can compensate you."

Arjun immediately made a note to check for a comprehensive **home insurance policy**.

Car Insurance: More Than Just a Legal Requirement

As the conversation continued, Eshwar moved on to another crucial topic—**car insurance**.

"You already have car insurance, right?" he asked.

"Yes, but just the basic one," Arjun replied.

"That's third-party insurance, which is mandatory," Eshwar explained. "But have you considered comprehensive insurance? If your car gets damaged in an accident, stolen, or destroyed in a flood, your basic insurance won't cover it."

Arjun had never thought about this. "So, a comprehensive plan covers both third-party liabilities and my own car's damages?"

"Yes, and it also includes add-ons like zero depreciation cover, engine protection, and roadside assistance," Eshwar said. "It may cost a little more, but in case of an accident, you won't have to pay a huge amount from your pocket."

Arjun remembered the time his colleague had to spend a fortune on repairs after his car was damaged in a flood. He decided to upgrade his policy to a **comprehensive car insurance plan**.

Business Insurance: Protecting Entrepreneurial Dreams

As they continued their discussion, Eshwar asked, "What about business owners? Do you think they need insurance?"

Arjun shrugged. "I suppose so. But I don't own a business, so I never really thought about it."

Eshwar leaned in. "Even if you don't, it's important to understand. Many entrepreneurs invest their life savings into their businesses. A fire, theft, or lawsuit could destroy everything overnight. Business insurance helps protect against such risks."

Arjun nodded. "So, what types of insurance should business owners consider?"

Eshwar listed them:

1. **Property Insurance** – Protects office buildings, factories, and equipment from fire, theft, and disasters.
2. **Liability Insurance** – Covers legal expenses if a customer sues for injury or product defects.
3. **Business Interruption Insurance** – Provides compensation if operations are halted due to unforeseen circumstances.

"Imagine running a factory and a fire destroys your machines," Eshwar explained. "Without insurance, you'd have to bear the full loss. But with proper coverage, you can recover and restart quickly."

Arjun thought about his friend who had opened a small restaurant recently. "Many people I know are starting businesses. This information could save them from financial ruin."

That evening, Arjun felt relieved knowing he was taking steps to **protect not just his life and health, but also his assets.** With home and car insurance in place, he had one less thing to worry about.

7. Common Mistakes People Make with Insurance

A few days after his discussion with Eshwar, Arjun decided to meet with his friend Vasu Dev over the weekend. They met at a café, where Vasu was busy checking his phone.

"Stock market updates?" Arjun asked, smiling.

Vasu laughed. "Always! But I was also reviewing my insurance policies. I'm trying to figure out if I need to make any changes."

Arjun was impressed. "That's great! I just started reviewing mine too. But tell me, what kind of policies do you have?"

Vasu leaned back. "Well, I have a life insurance policy that also gives me returns, and my car insurance is the basic one. Health insurance is covered by my company. That should be enough, right?"

Arjun hesitated. He remembered his conversation with Eshwar and sensed a few red flags. "I've been learning a lot about insurance lately. Mind if I share a few things?"

"Of course," Vasu said.

Arjun pulled out his notebook and began listing **common mistakes people make with insurance**—mistakes he had nearly made himself.

- **Buying Insurance as an Investment**

"You said your life insurance also gives you returns. Is it an endowment plan or ULIP?" Arjun asked.

Vasu nodded. "Yes, I think so. The agent told me I'll get a lump sum after 20 years."

Arjun sighed. "That's one of the biggest mistakes people make. Traditional life insurance plans like endowment and ULIPs mix investment with insurance. The problem? You get low coverage and low returns."

Vasu raised an eyebrow. "But it sounds like a good deal—insurance plus savings."

"Not really," Arjun explained. "The returns are often **less than 5% per year**, which is lower than what mutual funds or even PPF can offer. Plus, the life cover is tiny. If something happens to you, will   ₹10–15 lakh be enough for your family?"

Vasu's face fell. "I never thought of it that way."

"Instead, get a **pure term insurance** plan. It gives high coverage for low premiums. Invest separately in mutual funds or PPF for better returns."

• **Not Reviewing Coverage Regularly**

"Okay, I need to rethink my life insurance. What's the next mistake?" Vasu asked.

"Not reviewing coverage as your income and responsibilities grow," Arjun said. "Many people buy insurance once and forget about it."

Vasu thought for a moment. "That makes sense. I got my insurance five years ago when I was single. But now I'm married and planning a child. My financial needs have changed."

Arjun nodded. "Exactly! Your life cover should be **at least 10–15 times your annual income**. And health insurance should be upgraded as medical costs rise."

• **Underinsuring or Overinsuring**

"What about health insurance?" Vasu asked. "My company provides   ₹5 lakh coverage. Should I buy extra?"

"That depends," Arjun said. "   ₹5 lakh might have been enough a few years ago, but now a single hospital stay can cost that much. Ideally, you should have at least   **₹10–25 lakh** coverage, especially in a family floater plan."

Vasu frowned. "I never thought about medical inflation."

"Most people don't," Arjun said. "On the other hand, some people buy excessive coverage—like ₹2 crore health insurance—which they may never use. The key is **balance**."

- **Ignoring the Policy Fine Print**

"I hate reading insurance documents," Vasu admitted.

Arjun laughed. "You're not alone! But ignoring the fine print can be costly."

"What should I look out for?"

"Things like **waiting periods, exclusions, and claim procedures**," Arjun said. "For example, many health insurance plans don't cover pre-existing diseases for the first two or three years. And some term plans don't cover death due to certain reasons."

Vasu sighed. "So, I should read everything carefully before buying?"

"Absolutely. And clarify any doubts with the insurer."

- **Depending Only on Employer-Provided Insurance**

Vasu tapped his fingers on the table. "What about people who rely only on company health insurance?"

Arjun shook his head. "That's a mistake. What happens if you switch jobs or lose your job? The insurance is gone."

"That's true," Vasu admitted.

"To be safe, always have a **personal health insurance policy** in addition to your employer's coverage. This way, you're protected no matter what happens."

A Wake-Up Call for Vasu

By the time they finished their discussion, Vasu looked concerned. "I need to make changes. I'll get a term plan, upgrade my health cover, and check my existing policies."

Arjun smiled. "That's the goal—to avoid these common mistakes and protect yourself financially."

That night, as he walked home, Arjun felt proud. Not only was he securing his own future, but he was also helping his loved ones make better financial decisions.

8. Choosing the Right Insurance Plan

That evening, after his conversation with Vasu Dev, Arjun sat on the balcony, reflecting on everything he had learned about insurance. He had come a long way—from knowing little about financial protection to actively making informed decisions. But one question still nagged him: **How do I choose the right insurance plan?**

The next morning, Arjun met Eshwar at their usual spot in the park.

"You've made great progress," Eshwar said, noticing the thoughtful expression on Arjun's face. "But I sense there's still something on your mind."

Arjun nodded. "I understand the importance of insurance, but with so many options, how do I pick the right plan?"

Eshwar smiled. "Good question. Many people buy policies without proper evaluation and end up either underinsured or stuck with the wrong products. Let's break it down."

Compare Premium vs. Coverage – The Cheapest is Not Always the Best

Eshwar pulled out a notepad and drew two columns. In one, he wrote **Premium Amount**, and in the other, **Coverage Amount**.

"Many people choose the cheapest insurance policy available, thinking they've made a smart financial decision," he explained. "But cheaper isn't always better."

Arjun leaned in. "Why not?"

"Let's say one company offers you a **₹1 crore term insurance policy** for ₹8,000 per year, while another offers the same coverage for ₹6,500. You might be tempted to choose the lower premium. But what if the second company has a poor **claim settlement ratio?**"

Arjun frowned. "That means my family might struggle to get the claim amount if something happens to me?"

"Exactly," Eshwar said. "A slightly higher premium is worth it if the insurer has a good reputation and a smooth claim process."

Check the Claim Settlement Ratio

Arjun scribbled in his notebook: **Claim settlement ratio = Number of claims paid ÷ Number of claims received**.

"So, the higher the ratio, the better?"

"Yes," Eshwar confirmed. "Look for insurers with a claim settlement ratio of **above 95%**. This means they process most claims successfully, giving you peace of mind."

Arjun took out his phone. "Where do I check this?"

"Insurance Regulatory and Development Authority of India (**IRDAI**) publishes this data every year. Always check before buying a policy."

Opt for Sufficient Coverage

"Now," Eshwar continued, "let's talk about the right amount of coverage. For life insurance, you need at least **10–15 times your annual income.**"

Arjun did a quick calculation. "I earn ₹12 lakh per year. That means I should have at least ₹1.2 to ₹1.8

crore coverage?"

"Exactly. If you choose anything less, your family might struggle financially in your absence."

"What about health insurance?"

Eshwar nodded. "Medical costs are rising. Ideally, you should have at least ₹10–25 lakh coverage. If you're in a metro city, even ₹50 lakh might be necessary."

Arjun made a note. "What if I can't afford a high coverage policy?"

"You can take a base policy of ₹5–10 lakh and add a **top-up plan**. This way, you get higher coverage at a lower cost."

Disclose All Information Honestly

Eshwar's expression turned serious. "One mistake many people make is hiding health conditions to get lower premiums. That's a **big mistake**."

"Why?" Arjun asked.

"If you don't disclose pre-existing conditions, the insurer can reject your claim when you or your family need it the most. It's always better to be truthful."

Arjun nodded, making a mental note.

Arjun Takes Action

With this knowledge, Arjun decided to take the next step. That evening, he:

Compared different insurance policies online.
Checked claim settlement ratios on the IRDAI website.
Chose a ₹1.5 **crore term insurance policy** from a reputed insurer.
Upgraded his health insurance with a ₹15 **lakh family floater plan**.

As he clicked the **'Confirm'** button, he felt a wave of relief. For the first time, he knew his family's financial security was no longer a question mark.

9. Arjun's Action Plan for Financial Protection

A few days after selecting his insurance policies, Arjun sat in his study room, reviewing everything he had learned. His desk was filled with notes, comparison charts, and insurance brochures. It had been a journey—from being unaware of the risks his family faced to proactively securing their financial future.

As he sipped his coffee, Suneetha entered the room. "You've been so focused lately," she said, sitting beside him. "What's on your mind?"

Arjun smiled. "I finally feel like I've taken control of our financial security. Let me walk you through the plan."

Suneetha leaned in, listening carefully.

A. Securing the Family with Term Insurance

"The first thing I did was buy a **₹1.5 crore term insurance policy**," Arjun explained. "If anything happens to me, you and the kids will have enough money to maintain your lifestyle and cover major expenses like education and home loans."

Suneetha nodded. "That's a relief. But why term insurance? I heard about other plans that also give returns."

"Most of those policies have low coverage and high premiums," Arjun said. "Term insurance is pure protection. It's the most cost-effective way to secure our future."

B. Upgrading Health Insurance for Medical Emergencies

"Next," Arjun continued, "I realized that my company's health insurance isn't enough. So, I bought a **₹15 lakh family floater plan**."

Suneetha's eyes widened. "That makes sense. Medical costs are so high these days."

"Exactly. And I also added a **critical illness cover**, so we get a lump sum if something serious happens, like cancer or a heart attack."

"That's reassuring," Suneetha said, placing a hand on his.

C. Protecting Against Accidents and Disabilities

"Then I got a **personal accident insurance policy**," Arjun said. "If an accident leaves me permanently disabled, this will provide financial support."

Suneetha looked concerned. "I never thought about that. We always insure our car, but we never thought of insuring ourselves."

"Most people don't," Arjun admitted. "I also took a **disability insurance policy** to ensure we still have an income in case I can't work due to an injury."

D. Reviewing Asset Protection – Home and Car Insurance

"Next, I checked our existing insurance for our home and car," Arjun said. "Our car insurance is up to date, but I'm considering getting a **home insurance policy** to protect against fire, theft, or natural disasters."

"That's a good idea," Suneetha said. "We've worked so hard for this house. It's better to be safe."

E. Ensuring Regular Review of Policies

Arjun took out a notebook. "I created a system to review our insurance needs every year. Life changes—our income might grow, our expenses might change. We should update our policies accordingly."

Suneetha smiled. "You've thought of everything."

A Sense of Security

That evening, as they sat together, Arjun felt something he hadn't experienced in a long time—**peace of mind**.

For the first time, he was not just investing for wealth creation; he was protecting what truly mattered.

As he closed his notebook, he turned to Suneetha and said, "No matter what happens, our family will be financially secure. That's the best gift I can give."

Suneetha squeezed his hand. "And that's why I trust you."

The burden of uncertainty had been lifted. Arjun had built a safety net—not just for himself, but for the people he loved the most.

Chapter Conclusion

1. **Term Insurance** – ₹1.5 crore coverage to secure his family.
2. **Health Insurance** – ₹15 lakh family floater plan + critical illness cover.
3. **Accident & Disability Insurance** – To ensure financial protection in case of unforeseen events.
4. **Home & Car Insurance** – Reviewing and ensuring asset protection.
5. **Annual Review Plan** – To adjust coverage as life evolves.

CHAPTER THIRTEEN

When to Buy a House vs. Rent

1. The Emotional Dilemma

The evening breeze carried the scent of fresh paint and newly polished floors as Arjun and Suneetha stepped into the grand lobby of the newly launched apartment complex. The walls gleamed, the lighting was soft yet luxurious, and the sales manager greeted them with an eager smile.

"Sir, this is one of the best projects in the city. Premium amenities, great connectivity, and the price is only going to rise from here. A golden opportunity for early buyers!" the salesperson said enthusiastically.

Suneetha's eyes lit up as they walked through the model flat. The interiors were elegant, the kitchen was spacious, and the balcony overlooked a beautifully landscaped garden. She turned to Arjun with excitement.

"Isn't this perfect for us?" she whispered. "Our own home, no more shifting, no more landlords dictating rules. I can decorate it just the way I want!"

Arjun nodded but felt a familiar weight settle on his shoulders. He could see how much this meant to Suneetha. A house had always been a symbol of stability, of settling down, of success. But was this the right time? Was it the right decision for their finances?

The Pressure to Buy a Home

As they drove back home, Arjun found himself lost in thought. The idea of owning a house had been planted in his mind since childhood. His parents had always emphasized the importance of having a home.

"Renting is temporary, but owning a home is permanent," his father had often said.

At family gatherings, uncles and relatives would ask, "When are you buying your own place?" As if homeownership was the ultimate sign of adulthood and financial success.

His colleagues weren't helping either. Just last week, a friend at work had proudly shared how he had booked a 3BHK apartment, boasting about how property prices were skyrocketing.

"If you don't buy now, you'll regret it later. Prices only go up!" the friend had warned.

That night, as Arjun lay in bed, staring at the ceiling, he felt conflicted.

"Am I making a mistake by delaying buying a home?" he wondered.

The emotional pull was strong. The social pressure was real. But something in his gut told him to think it through.

A Conversation with Eshwar

The next day, Arjun met Eshwar over a cup of coffee. He laid out his thoughts, explaining how Suneetha wanted a home, how his family expected it, and how society viewed renting as a waste of money.

Eshwar listened patiently. Then, he leaned forward and said, "Arjun, buying a house is one of the biggest financial decisions in life. It should be based on **logic, not emotions**."

Arjun frowned. "But isn't owning a home a necessity? Isn't it an investment?"

Eshwar smiled. "That's exactly what we need to discuss. Before you decide, let's break down the myths and realities of homeownership. Because once you commit, you're in for decades of financial responsibility. Are you ready for that?"

Arjun took a deep breath and nodded. He knew this conversation could change his perspective forever.

2. The Common Myths About Homeownership

Eshwar leaned back, took a sip of his coffee, and smiled. "Alright, Arjun, let's start with the biggest myth that almost everyone believes."

Myth #1: 'Renting is a waste of money.'

Arjun nodded. "Isn't it? When I pay rent, I'm basically throwing money away. At least with an EMI, I'll own something in the end."

Eshwar shook his head. "That's what most people think, but let me ask you this—when you buy a house on loan, what do you think the EMI mostly covers in the first 10 years?"

Arjun thought for a moment. "Well, the loan amount..."

"No," Eshwar interrupted. "The major part of your EMI in the initial years goes toward **interest payments**, not the principal. So, for at least the first decade, you're mostly paying the bank's profit."

Arjun's eyes widened. "I never thought about it that way."

Eshwar continued, "Now, tell me—do you consider grocery expenses or electricity bills a waste of money?"

"Of course not," Arjun said. "Those are necessary expenses."

"Exactly," Eshwar said. "Rent is the same—it's the cost you pay for shelter. And in many cases, renting gives you flexibility without being tied down by a huge loan."

Myth #2: 'A home is always a good investment.'

Arjun folded his arms. "But property prices always go up, right?"

Eshwar chuckled. "That's another myth. Look at places like Japan or even parts of India—real estate prices have stagnated for years. Many cities have seen property prices rise, but they don't always beat inflation. In fact, the stock market has historically given better returns over long periods."

Arjun frowned. "But I've heard people say their house price doubled in ten years."

"Sure," Eshwar said. "But let's do some math. Say you buy a house for ₹1 crore. After 10 years, it appreciates to ₹2 crore. Sounds great, right?"

Arjun nodded.

"But what if I tell you that if you had invested ₹1 crore in a good mutual fund, you could have made ₹3-4 crore in the same time?"

Arjun's jaw dropped. "Wait... really?"

"Yes," Eshwar said. "Property appreciation isn't always as high as people assume. And don't forget the hidden costs—registration, maintenance, property tax, and interest on the loan. The real return is often much lower than people think."

Myth #3: 'Paying EMIs is better than paying rent.'

Arjun was still absorbing the previous point when Eshwar continued, "Now, about EMIs being better than rent. Let's assume you buy a house worth ₹1 crore. With a 20% down payment, you take an ₹80 lakh loan at 8% interest for 20 years. Can you guess your EMI?"

Arjun quickly calculated on his phone. "Around ₹ 67,000 per month."

"Correct. Now, how much rent do you pay for your current apartment?"

" ₹25,000," Arjun said.

Eshwar smiled. "Would you rather pay ₹67,000 and be stuck with a huge loan, or pay ₹25,000 and invest the difference?"

Arjun hesitated. "I never compared it like that."

"And don't forget," Eshwar added, "with an EMI, you're also paying interest, maintenance, and taxes. Your ₹ 67,000 EMI doesn't even include those!"

Myth #4: 'Owning a house means security.'

Arjun sighed. "Okay, but having a house gives stability, right? It's something I can pass on to my children."

Eshwar nodded. "That's true, but at what cost? If buying a home forces you into a financial struggle for 20 years, is that really security? True security comes from having enough savings, investments, and passive income to live comfortably."

He continued, "Besides, job security is uncertain these days. What if you buy a house in one city but get a better job offer somewhere else? A rented home gives you the flexibility to move."

Arjun leaned back in his chair, deep in thought. "So, you're saying that buying isn't always better than renting?"

"Exactly," Eshwar said. "It depends on your financial situation, your goals, and the numbers. That's why before making a decision, you need to consider the financial factors carefully."

Arjun nodded. "Alright, tell me—how do I decide if buying is right for me?"

Eshwar smiled. "Let's break it down step by step."

3. Financial Factors to Consider Before Buying

Eshwar leaned forward, sensing Arjun's curiosity. "Now that we've cleared up the myths, let's talk about the real factors that should influence your decision. Buying a house is not just about emotions—it's about financial preparedness. Here's what you must consider before making a decision."

A. Down Payment Readiness

"First and foremost, can you afford the down payment?" Eshwar asked.

Arjun hesitated. "I mean, I can arrange it. Maybe take some help from my parents or liquidate some investments."

Eshwar raised an eyebrow. "That's exactly what you **should not do**. You must be able to afford at least **20% of the property price** without depleting your savings. Otherwise, you're putting yourself in financial risk from day one."

He continued, "If you're buying a ₹1 crore house, you need ₹20 lakh for the down payment. But that's not all—you should still have an emergency fund of at least **6 months' expenses** after paying the down payment. If making the down payment leaves you with no savings, you're not ready."

Arjun sighed. "That makes sense. I was planning to use my entire savings for the down payment."

"That's a big mistake," Eshwar warned. "Many people do that and later regret it when unexpected expenses arise."

B. Loan EMI Burden

"Next, let's talk about the EMI," Eshwar said. "How much do you think is a safe EMI amount?"

Arjun shrugged. "As much as my salary allows?"

Eshwar shook his head. "Your **monthly EMIs should not exceed 30-40% of your income.** If you earn ₹1.5 lakh per month, your EMI should ideally be below ₹ 50,000- ₹60,000. Anything beyond that will strain your finances."

He continued, "Also, people forget that a home loan is a long-term commitment. **What if your income drops or unexpected expenses come up?** You must leave room for flexibility."

Arjun thought for a moment. "So, even if the bank approves a bigger loan, I should not take the maximum amount?"

"Exactly," Eshwar nodded. "Banks approve loans based on your current income, but they don't consider your future financial obligations. Just because the bank says you qualify for a ₹1 crore loan doesn't mean you should take it."

C. Hidden Costs of Homeownership

"Now, let's talk about the expenses people forget when buying a house," Eshwar said.

Arjun raised an eyebrow. "Like what?"

"Many hidden costs," Eshwar said, counting on his fingers:

- **Registration Fees & Stamp Duty**: Usually **5-7%** of the property price. So, for a ₹1 crore home, that's another ₹ 5-7 lakh.
- **Maintenance Charges**: Apartment maintenance fees can be **₹3,000-₹10,000 per month** or more.
- **Property Tax**: Every year, you must pay municipal property tax.

- **Home Insurance & Repairs**: Home insurance is an additional cost, and repairs can be unpredictable.

Arjun's eyes widened. "I didn't consider all this!"

"Most people don't," Eshwar said. "They assume the EMI is the only expense. But these hidden costs make homeownership more expensive than it seems."

D. Liquidity and Opportunity Cost

Eshwar leaned back and continued, "Now, here's something most homebuyers don't realize—when you put all your money into a house, your money is **locked**. It's not liquid."

Arjun frowned. "But I can always sell the house, right?"

Eshwar shook his head. "Real estate is **not** a liquid asset. Selling a house takes time—sometimes months or years. If you suddenly need cash, you can't just withdraw money like you would from a mutual fund."

He added, "Also, when you put   ₹1 crore into a house, you lose the **opportunity** to invest it elsewhere—like stocks or mutual funds—that might give you better returns."

Arjun scratched his head. "I never thought of that. So, buying a house isn't just about the price—it's about what else I could do with that money."

"Exactly," Eshwar said. "That's called **opportunity cost**. You must ask yourself: 'If I don't buy this house, can I use this money to make better returns elsewhere?'"

E. Investment Perspective

Arjun sighed. "So, is real estate not a good investment at all?"

Eshwar smiled. "It **can** be—if you buy at the right price and location. But in many cases, stocks or mutual funds give better returns over the long term."

He continued, "For example, the **Sensex has historically grown at 12-15% per year**. Compare that to real estate, which grows at 6-8% on average. Over 20 years, stock market investments often outperform property investments."

Arjun frowned. "But I thought property prices always increase?"

"Not always," Eshwar said. "Real estate is **not** a guaranteed high-return investment. It depends on **location, demand, and economic factors**. Many people assume their house will double in value, but that's not always true."

The Decision Framework

Eshwar leaned forward. "So, before buying a house, you must ask yourself these questions:"

1. **Can I afford the down payment without depleting my savings?**
2. **Is my EMI within 30-40% of my income?**
3. **Have I accounted for all hidden costs like maintenance and property tax?**
4. **Will I have enough liquidity for emergencies after buying the house?**
5. **Am I missing out on better investment opportunities by locking money into real estate?**

"If you can confidently answer **YES** to all these, then buying might be a good decision for you," Eshwar concluded.

Arjun nodded slowly, absorbing all the information. "This is a completely different way of looking at home buying. I need to rethink everything."

Eshwar smiled. "That's the goal—to make decisions based on **facts, not emotions**. Now, let's look at when renting makes more sense."

4. When Renting Makes More Sense

Arjun sat back, still processing everything Eshwar had said. "So, if buying a house isn't always the best decision, when does renting make more sense?"

Eshwar smiled. "That's a great question, Arjun. Renting is often the smarter financial choice in many situations. Let's go through the reasons one by one."

1. When Rent is Significantly Lower Than EMI Costs

Eshwar picked up a pen and drew two simple calculations on a notepad.

"Let's say you want to buy a 2BHK apartment that costs ₹1 crore. The EMI for a home loan at 8% interest for 20 years would be around **₹80,000 per month**."

Arjun nodded. "That sounds about right."

"Now, let's compare that to renting. A similar apartment might have a monthly rent of **₹25,000**."

Arjun raised an eyebrow. "That's a huge difference!"

"Exactly," Eshwar said. "If you rent instead of buying, you save **₹55,000 per month**. Now, imagine you invest that ₹55,000 in mutual funds or stocks, earning **12-15% per year**. Over 20 years, that investment could grow to several crores!"

Arjun leaned forward. "So renting actually gives me the chance to grow my wealth instead of locking it in a house?"

"Yes," Eshwar nodded. "Many people don't realize that buying a house means losing the opportunity to invest that money elsewhere."

2. When Job Location is Uncertain

Eshwar continued, "Think about this—how long do you plan to stay in this city?"

Arjun hesitated. "I'm not sure. If I get a better job opportunity elsewhere, I might move."

"That's another reason why renting makes sense," Eshwar said. "Buying a house **ties you down to one location**. If you need to relocate for work, selling a house is difficult, and renting it out comes with its own hassles."

Arjun sighed. "That's true. A few of my friends bought houses, but when they got jobs in different cities, they struggled to sell or rent out their flats."

"Exactly," Eshwar said. "Renting gives you **mobility and flexibility**. You can move whenever you want without worrying about selling a property."

3. When Real Estate Prices are Stagnant or Overvalued

Eshwar picked up his phone and opened a property website. "Look at this—some cities have seen very little price appreciation in the last five years."

Arjun glanced at the numbers. "So, buying in these areas wouldn't be a good investment?"

"Correct," Eshwar said. "If property prices are not rising significantly, you're better off renting and investing your money elsewhere."

He continued, "Many people assume real estate always goes up, but that's not true. In some cities, property prices stay flat for years, while in others, they grow too slowly to justify the investment."

Arjun nodded. "So I need to check the historical price trends before even considering buying."

"Yes," Eshwar agreed. "If real estate prices are stagnant, renting is the better financial decision."

4. When Investing the Difference Can Generate Higher Returns

Eshwar smiled. "This is the most important point—**if you rent instead of buying, you can invest the difference and potentially generate much higher returns.**"

Arjun leaned in. "Give me an example."

"Alright," Eshwar said, grabbing his notepad again. "Let's say you rent a house for ₹25,000 instead of paying an ₹80,000 EMI. That means you have **₹55,000 per month** available for investing."

He continued, "If you invest ₹55,000 every month in an index fund or mutual fund that gives an **average return of 12% per year**, guess how much money you will have in **20 years?**"

Arjun thought for a moment. "A few crores?"

Eshwar smiled. "More than that. You'll have **₹5.5 crore!**"

Arjun's jaw dropped. "Seriously? Just by investing the money I save from renting?"

"Yes," Eshwar said. "Now, compare this with buying a house. After 20 years, your house may be worth **₹2-3 crore**, but you would have also paid **huge interest on the loan**. In the end, renting and investing might give you a better financial outcome."

Arjun's Realization

Arjun took a deep breath. "I never thought about it this way. All my life, I believed that owning a house was the ultimate goal."

Eshwar nodded. "That's because society tells us that renting is a waste of money. But in reality, renting gives you financial flexibility, allows you to invest in higher-return assets, and gives you the freedom to move whenever needed."

Arjun rubbed his chin. "So renting is not just about avoiding debt—it's actually a strategic financial decision?"

"Exactly," Eshwar said. "Renting is often **the smarter choice for wealth creation**, especially if your job location is uncertain, real estate prices are stagnant, or you can invest the savings in higher-return assets."

Arjun sat silently, absorbing everything. "I think I need to rethink my entire approach to homeownership."

Eshwar smiled. "That's the goal—make decisions **based on financial logic, not just emotions or societal pressure.**"

5. When Buying a House is a Good Decision

Arjun leaned back in his chair, still deep in thought. "So, renting makes sense in many cases. But surely, buying a house must also have its advantages, right?"

Eshwar nodded. "Of course. Owning a home can be a great decision—if done at the right time and under the right conditions. Let's look at when buying actually makes sense."

A. When You Have Financial Stability

Eshwar placed a firm hand on Arjun's shoulder. "The first rule of buying a house is simple—**never buy if your financial situation is unstable.**"

"What do you mean?" Arjun asked.

"You should only consider buying if:"

- **You have a steady and secure income.** A home loan is a long-term commitment, so your cash flow should be predictable.
- **You don't have major existing loans.** If you already have large EMIs for a car or personal loan, adding a home loan will overburden you.
- **Your emergency fund is intact.** Even after making a down payment, you should have 6-12 months of

expenses saved for unexpected situations.

Arjun frowned. "A lot of people take huge home loans without thinking about this."

"Exactly," Eshwar said. "That's why so many people struggle with EMIs and financial stress. Buying a house should only happen when you have **complete financial stability**."

B. When the House is for Long-Term Living

Eshwar took out a pen and underlined the words "**Long-Term**" on his notepad.

"A house is a long-term commitment," he explained. "You should only buy if you plan to stay in it for at least **10-15 years**."

"Why is that?" Arjun asked.

"Because buying a house involves high costs—registration fees, stamp duty, maintenance, and loan interest. If you sell within a few years, you might **not even recover these costs**, let alone make a profit."

Arjun nodded. "So, buying makes sense only if I'm sure I'll stay there for a long time?"

"Exactly," Eshwar said. "If there's a chance you'll move in the next 5 years, renting is the better option."

C. When the Loan EMIs are Affordable

Eshwar pulled out his phone calculator. "Let's say you're earning ₹1.5 lakh per month. Do you think taking a home loan with a ₹1.2 lakh EMI is a good idea?"

Arjun laughed. "Of course not! That's almost my entire salary."

"Exactly. A safe rule is: **Your home loan EMI should not exceed 30-40% of your monthly income**."

Arjun thought for a moment. "But many people take loans where EMIs eat up more than half their salary."

"That's financial suicide," Eshwar said seriously. "You should still have enough money left for savings, investments, and emergencies. If an EMI is too high, it **traps you in a financial cage.**"

"So, if the EMI is too high, I should either wait or buy a more affordable house?" Arjun asked.

"Correct," Eshwar said. "Buying should not come at the cost of your financial peace."

D. When the Price-to-Rent Ratio is Favorable

"Arjun, do you remember the **Price-to-Rent Ratio** we discussed?"

"Yes," Arjun said. "It's the property price divided by the annual rent. If the ratio is above 20, renting is better. If it's below 15, buying is better."

"Exactly," Eshwar said. "Before buying, always check this ratio. If property prices are too high compared to rent, then it's better to wait or rent instead."

Arjun made a note. "So, buying is a smart decision only when the price makes sense mathematically, not just emotionally?"

"Correct," Eshwar smiled. "We should **buy based on logic, not just desire.**"

E. When Emotional Factors Matter

Eshwar leaned back. "Now, while finances are the most important factor, we can't ignore emotions."

Arjun raised an eyebrow. "But didn't you say decisions should be logical?"

"Yes, but logic doesn't mean ignoring your feelings," Eshwar said. "There are situations where buying a home makes sense **because of personal reasons.**"

- **If you want stability for your family.** If you have kids, owning a home gives them a stable environment without worrying about moving frequently.

- **If you want to customize your living space.** Renting means you can't make major changes to the property.
- **If you value emotional security over financial calculations.** Some people feel happier and more at peace owning their own home.

Arjun thought for a moment. "So, if I can afford it without financial strain, and I really want to settle down, then buying makes sense?"

"Yes," Eshwar said. "The key is to make sure emotions don't **override financial wisdom**. You should be able to afford it comfortably, not struggle to maintain it."

Arjun's Realization

Arjun sat back and sighed. "So, the answer is not black and white. Renting is sometimes better, and buying is sometimes better. It all depends on my financial situation and future plans."

"Exactly," Eshwar said. "There is no universal rule. The right decision is different for everyone."

Arjun smiled. "I feel much clearer now. Instead of blindly following what society says, I'll make a choice based on what truly works for me."

"That's the spirit," Eshwar said. "Financial freedom comes from making **smart, well-thought-out decisions**, not just following the crowd."

Arjun looked at his notes. "I'll analyze my finances carefully before making any decision. And if I rent, I'll make sure to invest the savings wisely."

Eshwar grinned. "Now you're thinking like a true wealth builder!"

6. The Price-to-Rent Ratio – A Simple Calculation

The next morning, Arjun sat in his study, sipping his coffee while running some numbers. The previous night's discussion with Eshwar had been eye-opening. He realized that most people around him bought houses without understanding the actual financial impact.

Just then, Eshwar called. "Arjun, have you thought about the price-to-rent ratio we discussed?"

"Yes," Arjun replied. "I understand the concept, but I need help applying it to real-world numbers."

"Great! Let's go through an example together," Eshwar said.

Understanding the Price-to-Rent Ratio

"The price-to-rent ratio is simple," Eshwar explained. "It's calculated using this formula:"

$$\text{Price-to-Rent Ratio} = \frac{\text{Property Price}}{\text{Annual Rent}}$$

"If the ratio is **below 15**, buying makes sense. If it's **above 20**, renting is better. Anything between 15-20 depends on your financial goals and stability."

Arjun grabbed a notepad. "Let's take a real example. Say an apartment costs ₹1 crore, and the monthly rent for a similar apartment is ₹30,000."

"Perfect," Eshwar said. "Now calculate the annual rent."

$$\text{Annual Rent} = 30,000 \times 12 = 3,60,000$$

"Now, divide the property price by the annual rent:"

$$\frac{1,00,00,000}{3,60,000} \approx 27.8$$

Arjun's eyes widened. "That's way above 20!"

"Exactly," Eshwar said. "With a ratio of **27.8**, renting is the smarter choice."

What Does This Ratio Tell Us?

Arjun leaned back. "So, this means the house is overvalued?"

"Not necessarily," Eshwar said. "It just means that, financially, renting is a **better deal** right now. Instead of locking up   ₹1 crore in a property, you could rent the same home for   ₹30,000 and invest the remaining money for higher returns."

"But what if the ratio was 12 or 14?" Arjun asked.

"In that case, buying could be a good decision," Eshwar replied. "It means the price is reasonable compared to the rent. But even then, you should check affordability, location stability, and long-term plans."

Arjun nodded. "And if it's between 15 and 20?"

"Then it depends on personal preference," Eshwar said. "Some people may prefer to buy for security, while others may rent and invest the difference. But if the ratio is way above 20, it's usually a sign that real estate prices are inflated."

Testing the Formula for Different Locations

Arjun was intrigued. "Can we check this ratio for different cities?"

"Of course," Eshwar said. "For example, in smaller towns, home prices are lower, and rent is also lower. The ratio might be **around 10-15**, making buying a good option. But in metro cities like Mumbai, Bangalore, or Hyderabad, the ratio is often **above 25**, making renting the better choice."

Arjun thought about his own city. "So, before deciding, I should check the property price and rent ratio in my area?"

"Absolutely!" Eshwar said. "This one formula can help you **avoid costly mistakes.**"

7. Alternative Investment Options

Arjun had another question. "If I decide to rent instead of buying, what should I do with the money I save?"

Eshwar smiled. "Great question! Most people forget that renting saves money, which can be **invested wisely.**"

"Here are some better alternatives to investing your capital instead of buying a house:"

A. Investing in Stocks and Mutual Funds

✓ **Equity Mutual Funds** – Over long periods, stock market investments **give higher returns** than real estate. Historically, equity markets have delivered **12-15% annual returns**, compared to **6-8% in real estate.**

✓ **Index Funds** – Simple, low-cost investments in the stock market that grow wealth over time.

✓ **SIP (Systematic Investment Plan)** – Instead of paying EMI, invest monthly in mutual funds for **compounded growth.**

Arjun was surprised. "I never compared stock market returns to real estate before!"

"That's why most people assume a house is their best investment," Eshwar said. "But in reality, **stocks often outperform real estate** over the long run."

B. REITs (Real Estate Investment Trusts)

✓ Instead of buying a house, you can invest in **REITs,** which allow you to own a share in real estate projects without buying an entire property.

✓ REITs provide **rental income** and appreciation, just like physical property, but with **less hassle** and **more liquidity.**

C. Building a Diversified Portfolio

✓ Instead of putting **all** money into one house, Arjun could **diversify** his investments across stocks, bonds, gold, and real estate investment trusts.

✓ A well-diversified portfolio reduces risk and **ensures financial freedom** faster than locking money into real estate.

Arjun was impressed. "So, renting doesn't just give flexibility, it also allows me to build wealth faster?"

"Exactly!" Eshwar grinned. "It's all about using money **wisely** instead of following traditional thinking."

8. Arjun's Decision

That evening, Arjun and Suneetha sat together, going over the numbers.

Suneetha sighed. "I always thought owning a home meant security, but now I see it's not always the best choice financially."

Arjun smiled. "Yes. We were almost about to take a **huge loan** without checking if it made sense!"

"So, what should we do?" she asked.

"For now, we'll **continue renting** and invest the savings into stocks and mutual funds," Arjun said confidently.

Suneetha nodded. "That sounds like a smart plan. We'll buy a home **only when it makes financial sense**."

Arjun felt a sense of relief. For the first time, he was making a financial decision **based on logic, not pressure**.

Eshwar's words echoed in his mind:

"Financial security doesn't come from just owning a home—it comes from owning assets that generate wealth."

Arjun smiled. This was the beginning of his journey to true financial freedom.

Key Takeaways from This Chapter

- **Buying a house should be a financial decision, not an emotional one.**
- **Use the Price-to-Rent Ratio** to evaluate whether renting or buying is better.
- **Renting is often smarter when home prices are too high** compared to rent.
- **Investing in stocks and mutual funds** can generate higher returns than real estate.
- **Financial freedom comes from growing wealth, not just homeownership.**

Arjun had learned a powerful lesson: **The goal is not just to own a house—the goal is to achieve financial independence.**

CHAPTER FOURTEEN

The psychology of Money

1. Why Smart People Make Dumb Money Decisions

It was a lazy Sunday afternoon, and Arjun sat in his study, flipping through the pages of a book on investing. His eyes landed on a startling statistic: **More than 80% of investors lose money in the stock market despite having access to the same knowledge and tools as successful investors.**

He frowned. "If knowledge is easily available, why do so many people still fail?" he wondered aloud.

Just then, Eshwar called.

"Deep in thought, Arjun?" Eshwar's voice was lighthearted.

"Yes, Eshwar! I was reading about how most investors lose money, even when they have all the data, charts, and strategies at their fingertips. It doesn't make sense!"

Eshwar chuckled. "That's because **your mind, not your math, determines your wealth.**"

Arjun was intrigued. "What do you mean?"

"Let me ask you something—why do people, despite knowing that eating junk food is bad for health, still indulge in it?"

Arjun smiled. "Because it's tempting! And habits are hard to break."

"Exactly!" Eshwar said. "When it comes to money, the same behavioral patterns control our decisions. Financial success isn't just about numbers; **it's about controlling emotions.** And emotions lead people to make the biggest money mistakes."

The Three Deadly Money Mistakes

Eshwar continued, "There are three major emotional traps that even the smartest people fall into when dealing with money: **Greed, Fear, and Ego.**"

a. Greed—The FOMO Trap

"Do you remember the time you bought that penny stock because everyone in your WhatsApp group was talking about it?" Eshwar asked with a teasing tone.

Arjun laughed nervously. "Yes... I thought I was missing out on a great opportunity!"

"And what happened?"

"It crashed within weeks. I lost half my money!"

Eshwar nodded. "That's **Greed**, Arjun. When people hear about others making money quickly, they jump in without thinking. This is called **FOMO—Fear of Missing Out.** It's the same reason people buy stocks at their peak and get trapped."

"But Eshwar, how do successful investors avoid this?"

"They don't let **hype** control them," Eshwar said. "Instead of chasing trends, they focus on **fundamentals and long-term gains.** If you feel the urge to buy something just because everyone else is buying, take a step back. Ask yourself, *Is this truly a good investment, or am I just afraid of missing out?*"

Arjun nodded. "I've definitely fallen into this trap before. I need to train myself to think rationally."

b. Fear—The Panic Selling Mistake

Arjun sighed, remembering another bad decision. "You know, during the last market crash, I panicked and sold most of my stocks at a loss."

Eshwar smiled knowingly. "Ah, **Fear—the second biggest money destroyer.** When markets fall, the news spreads panic, and people sell out of fear. But tell me, Arjun, what happened to those stocks later?"

Arjun hesitated. "Well... they actually recovered, and some even went higher than before!"

"Exactly! If you had just **stayed invested**, you wouldn't have lost money. The stock market moves in cycles. **Crashes are temporary, but growth is permanent.**"

Arjun sighed. "So, the lesson is to stay calm and not let fear take over?"

"Yes!" Eshwar said. "The best investors don't react emotionally. They **see market crashes as opportunities** to buy good stocks at cheaper prices instead of selling in panic."

c. Ego—The Cost of Not Admitting Mistakes

Arjun frowned. "I've seen people hold on to bad stocks for years, hoping they will recover, even when the company is clearly failing."

Eshwar nodded. "That's because of **Ego.** People hate admitting they made a mistake. Instead of cutting losses early, they hold on, hoping the price will come back."

"But doesn't that just increase losses?"

"Exactly!" Eshwar said. "A smart investor knows when to admit they're wrong and **move on.**"

Arjun thought for a moment. "So, to succeed in investing, I must control Greed, Fear, and Ego?"

"Yes! **Mastering emotions is more important than mastering the stock market.** The real battle is in the mind."

Arjun smiled. "This changes everything, Eshwar. I thought investing was just about knowledge and strategies. But now I see that **controlling emotions is the real secret.**"

Eshwar patted his shoulder. "You're on the right path, Arjun. And this is just the beginning."

2. The Power of Delayed Gratification

Arjun was enjoying his morning coffee while browsing investment articles on his tablet when he came across a story about a young professional who squandered his entire salary on luxuries, leaving nothing for investments. He shook his head and muttered, **"Financial discipline is everything."**

That evening, as he met Eshwar for their usual walk in the park, he brought up the topic.

"Eshwar, I read an article today about how people struggle with impulse spending. I've always been mindful of my finances, but sometimes, I wonder—how do I ensure I never fall into that trap?"

Eshwar smiled. "That's a great question, Arjun. Even the most disciplined people can be tested when temptation strikes. But do you know what separates those who build wealth from those who don't?"

Arjun pondered for a moment. "I'd say... **controlling desires and thinking long-term.**"

"Exactly!" Eshwar nodded. "Let me share an interesting psychological experiment with you."

The Marshmallow Experiment – A Lesson in Self-Control

Eshwar pulled out his phone and showed Arjun a short clip.

"In this study, young kids were given a choice: eat one marshmallow immediately or wait 15 minutes and get two marshmallows instead."

Arjun chuckled. "I remember reading about this. The kids who waited ended up being more successful in life, right?"

"Correct! The ability to delay gratification leads to **better financial decisions, stronger self-control, and long-term success.**"

"That makes perfect sense," Arjun said. "I follow the same principle when it comes to money. If I can invest ₹ 1,00,000 today instead of spending it, I'd rather watch it grow over time."

"That's the right mindset, Arjun. But the real test is when opportunities or temptations come disguised as 'rewards.'"

The Wealthy vs. The Impulsive

Eshwar continued, "The wealthy aren't rich because they earn huge salaries. They're rich because they **master the art of waiting.** They delay luxuries until their investments can comfortably afford them."

Arjun nodded. "I've always believed in letting my money work for me. I don't mind waiting for the things I want, as long as my investments are growing."

"That's the key," Eshwar said. "People often think wealth is about making more money. But in reality, it's about **making smart choices with the money you already have.**"

Invest First, Spend Later

Eshwar leaned in. "Here's a golden rule: **Buy luxuries from investment returns, not from your salary.**"

Arjun's face lit up. "I love that! So, instead of using my active income for expensive things, I should let my investments generate passive income and spend from that?"

"Exactly! When your assets start paying for your desires, you've truly achieved financial freedom."

Arjun smiled. "I guess I've been on the right path. But this conversation just reinforced my conviction—building wealth is all about the **right habits.**"

Eshwar patted his back. "Indeed, Arjun. **Discipline today creates abundance tomorrow.**"

3. Loss Aversion—Why Losses Hurt More Than Gains

One evening, Arjun and Eshwar were sipping tea at their favorite café when the conversation turned to market downturns.

"You know, Eshwar," Arjun said, stirring his tea thoughtfully, "I've noticed something about myself. Even though I have a solid investment plan, I still feel a sharp sting when my portfolio dips—even temporarily. It's irrational, but losses feel more intense than gains."

Eshwar chuckled. "Welcome to the psychology of money! That feeling has a name—it's called **loss aversion.** Our minds are wired to experience losses much more painfully than the joy of an equivalent gain."

Arjun raised an eyebrow. "So even if I gain ₹1 lakh over a year but lose ₹50,000 in a single month, my mind focuses more on the loss?"

"Exactly," Eshwar nodded. "Imagine this: You're walking in the park and someone hands you ₹500. Feels good, right?"

Arjun smiled. "Of course!"

"Now, imagine you're walking again, but this time, **₹ 500 slips from your pocket and you lose it.**"

Arjun frowned. "That would definitely feel worse than the happiness of getting ₹500 for free."

"And that, my friend, is loss aversion at work," Eshwar said. "We tend to react more strongly to losing something than to gaining the same amount."

How Loss Aversion Affects Investing

Arjun leaned back in his chair. "That explains why so many investors panic and sell during market crashes."

"Absolutely," Eshwar agreed. "Even seasoned investors aren't immune to this. Some people sell great stocks during corrections, fearing further losses, only to regret it later."

Arjun nodded. "I've trained myself to stay calm, but I won't deny that seeing red in my portfolio still affects me emotionally."

"That's natural," Eshwar assured him. "But here's the trick: **Reframe how you view losses.** Instead of seeing them as failures, see them as part of the process. Every investor, even the best, faces drawdowns. What matters is how you respond."

Developing a Resilient Investor Mindset

"Alright," Arjun said, "so how do I train my mind to handle losses better?"

"Three things," Eshwar said, holding up his fingers.

a. Focus on the bigger picture: Instead of reacting to daily price swings, zoom out. Look at a 5- or 10-year chart of successful companies. The trend is upward despite short-term dips.

b. Set predefined rules: Decide in advance what level of loss is acceptable before you invest. That way, emotions won't dictate your decisions.

c. Learn from history: The market has seen countless crashes, but it has **always recovered and grown over time.** Smart investors buy more during downturns instead of selling in fear.

Arjun took a deep breath. "That makes a lot of sense. I've always known markets recover, but now I see that controlling my emotions is just as important as picking good investments."

Eshwar smiled. "That's why investing is more of a psychological game than a numbers game. **The best investors aren't the smartest ones—they're the ones who master their emotions.**"

Arjun nodded. "From now on, I'll see temporary losses as opportunities rather than threats."

4. The Danger of Lifestyle Inflation

One afternoon, Arjun and Suneetha were discussing their future plans over lunch. Arjun had recently received a significant salary hike, and Suneetha was excited about the possibilities.

"We've worked hard for this, Arjun. Maybe it's time to upgrade a few things—a bigger car, a better house, a vacation abroad?" she suggested, scrolling through pictures of luxurious destinations on her phone.

Arjun smiled, understanding her enthusiasm. "I get what you're saying, Suneetha. We can afford these things now, but do we really need them?"

She raised an eyebrow. "Come on, Arjun. We deserve a better lifestyle. We shouldn't have to think twice about spending now."

Arjun leaned back and took a thoughtful pause. "That's the trap many high earners fall into—**lifestyle inflation.** As income grows, so do expenses, and before they know it, they're stuck in a cycle where no amount of money feels enough."

Suneetha frowned. "But what's wrong with enjoying the money we've earned?"

"Nothing is wrong with enjoying it," Arjun reassured her. "But let me put it this way—imagine we start spending more on luxury cars, vacations, and dining out. Over time, these become our new normal, right?"

Suneetha nodded.

"Now, what happens if my income stops growing at the same pace? Or worse, if something unexpected happens, like job loss or a recession?"

Suneetha hesitated. "We'd feel the pinch because we'd already adjusted to a higher level of spending."

"Exactly," Arjun said. "That's why many people, despite earning crores, live paycheck to paycheck. Their expenses grow just as fast as their income, leaving them financially vulnerable."

How Arjun Manages Lifestyle Inflation

"But Arjun," Suneetha asked, "how do you balance enjoying life today while securing our future?"

Arjun smiled. "It's all about setting priorities. Here's what I follow:"

a. Save and Invest First, Spend Later:

"Whenever my income increases, I don't immediately increase my spending. Instead, I increase my investments first."

b. Upgrade with a Purpose:

"If we upgrade our car or home, it should be because it adds value to our lives, not just to impress others."

c. Keep Fixed Expenses Low:

"Many people commit to high EMIs thinking their income will always grow. I avoid unnecessary long-term financial burdens."

4. Enjoy, but Within Limits:

"We'll take vacations, dine out, and buy nice things—but within a budget that keeps us financially secure."

Suneetha nodded. "That actually makes sense. No point in earning more if we just end up spending it all. So, how do we decide what's a reasonable upgrade?"

"Simple," Arjun said. "Before making any big financial decision, we ask—**Will this make us wealthier or just**

make us look wealthier?"

Suneetha smiled. "I like that. Let's plan a vacation—but a smart one that doesn't derail our financial goals."

Arjun laughed. "Now that's the mindset of true financial freedom!"

5. The Role of Habits in Wealth Creation

It was a quiet evening, and Arjun sat on his balcony, sipping his favorite green tea. His mind wandered back to his journey—from struggling to save in his early career to now managing his finances with ease. Eshwar's voice echoed in his mind:

"Wealth isn't built by one big decision—it's built by the habits you repeat every day."

As he reflected, Suneetha walked in. "Deep in thought again?" she teased, sitting beside him.

Arjun chuckled. "Just thinking about how financial success is really just a series of small, smart decisions over time."

She raised an eyebrow. "Like what?"

Arjun's Wealth-Building Habits

Arjun took a deep breath and listed out the habits that transformed his financial life:

a. Tracking Expenses Without Fail

"I've made it a habit to review our expenses weekly. It's not about restricting spending, but about knowing where our money goes. If we don't track it, we can't improve it."

Suneetha smiled. "That's true. Ever since we started tracking, I've noticed we spend a lot less on impulse purchases."

b. Automating Savings and Investments

"I don't wait till the end of the month to save. The moment my salary is credited, a fixed amount is automatically invested. This way, we never 'forget' to save."

Suneetha nodded. "I used to think saving what's left after spending was enough, but now I see why we should save first and spend later."

c. Reading and Learning About Finance Daily

"Every day, I spend at least 20–30 minutes learning something new about finance—reading books, listening to podcasts, or analyzing investment strategies. The more I learn, the better decisions I make."

Suneetha laughed. "No wonder you always have something new to tell me about money!"

d. Avoiding Get-Rich-Quick Traps

"I've trained myself to ignore any investment that sounds too good to be true. Whether it's high-return schemes, penny stocks, or crypto hype—if it promises quick riches, it's usually a trap."

Suneetha sighed. "Remember when my friend got lured into that Ponzi scheme? She lost so much money."

Arjun nodded. "That's why discipline is key. If we follow solid, proven strategies consistently, we'll achieve financial freedom without unnecessary risks."

Building a Wealth Mindset

Suneetha rested her head on Arjun's shoulder. "So, it's not just about earning more, but about being disciplined with what we earn?"

"Exactly," Arjun said. "Financial freedom isn't about luck or one-time windfalls—it's about daily habits. Wealth isn't built overnight, but with steady, consistent actions."

Suneetha smiled. "I like this version of us. We're not just making money—we're making money work for us."

Arjun grinned. "That's the goal. And if we stay consistent, financial freedom is just a matter of time."

6. Handling Financial Stress and Uncertainty

It was late at night, and the house was silent except for the faint hum of the ceiling fan. Arjun was wide awake, not from worry but from contemplation.

Suneetha turned to him. "Thinking about something?"

Arjun smiled. "Not exactly worried, but I was reflecting on how even the most well-planned finances can be tested by uncertainty—market fluctuations, unexpected expenses, or economic downturns. I've put safeguards in place, but I always believe in refining my approach."

Suneetha nodded. "You always plan ahead, and that's what gives me peace of mind. But let's be honest, not everyone does. Even among our friends, many are earning well but live paycheck to paycheck."

Arjun sighed. "That's true. Financial stability isn't just about earning—it's about being prepared for the unexpected."

Eshwar's Perspective on True Financial Stability

The next day, Arjun met Eshwar for their usual morning walk. He shared his thoughts, and Eshwar listened attentively.

"Arjun, you're one of the few people I know who doesn't just earn well but also thinks ahead. You already have financial safety nets in place. But let's go beyond just individual preparation—let's talk about the mindset that truly removes financial stress."

Arjun was intrigued. "I'm listening."

a. Emergency Fund: The Mental Comfort Factor

Eshwar smiled. "You've built a strong emergency fund. But tell me, do you see it just as a financial tool, or does it serve a bigger purpose?"

Arjun thought for a moment. "It's more than just money in a bank—it's mental security. Knowing that no matter what happens, my family's basic needs are covered for a year gives me the freedom to take calculated risks."

Eshwar nodded. "Exactly! Many people think an emergency fund is just a financial buffer. But the real benefit is that it stops you from making emotional decisions—like panic-selling investments or taking bad loans in desperation."

b. Market Crashes: A Master's Perspective

"Last time the markets dipped, I noticed some of my friends were selling in panic," Arjun said. "I, on the other hand, saw it as an opportunity and bought more."

Eshwar laughed. "That's the difference between a seasoned investor and a reactive one. The market doesn't reward emotions—it rewards patience and strategy."

- **Market downturns are opportunities, not threats.**
- **Those who stay calm and invest during crashes often build generational wealth.**
- **Emotional detachment from market fluctuations is a key trait of financial masters.**

c. Future-Proofing Income: Thinking Beyond the Paycheck

Arjun took a sip of his coffee. "A lot of people rely solely on their salary, which makes job security a major stress factor. I've always believed in diversifying income sources."

Eshwar smiled. "And that's why you're ahead. The people who stress about job loss the most are those who have no Plan B. Wealth is not just what you earn—it's how many income sources you build."

- **Passive income streams (investments, rentals, businesses) reduce reliance on a single paycheck.**

- **Continuous skill development ensures employability in any market condition.**
- **Thinking like an entrepreneur—finding ways to make money work for you—is key.**

Arjun nodded. "That's why I've ensured that even if I stop working for a year, my investments will take care of expenses."

d. The Role of Financial Clarity in Relationships

That evening, as Arjun and Suneetha sat on their balcony, she said, "You know, financial stress ruins so many relationships. I've seen couples fight over expenses, debts, and future goals."

Arjun leaned back in his chair. "That's because many couples don't treat financial planning as teamwork. You and I have always been open about our financial goals, and that transparency removes stress."

- **Having clear, shared financial goals strengthens relationships.**
- **Open conversations about money prevent misunderstandings.**
- **Building wealth together fosters trust and unity.**

Suneetha smiled. "That's why I never worry about money—I know we're always aligned in our approach."

e. The Final Ingredient: Emotional Mastery Over Money

Eshwar's parting words stayed with Arjun:

"True financial freedom isn't just about numbers—it's about mastering your emotions around money."

Arjun already had financial security, but what set him apart was his mindset—he saw money as a tool, not a source of stress. He understood that the real wealth wasn't just in his bank balance, but in his ability to remain calm, think long-term, and make decisions based on logic, not fear.

As he watched the city lights twinkle in the distance, Arjun knew—he wasn't just financially secure; he was financially unshakable.

The Importance of a Money Mindset

As Arjun sipped his evening tea, he reflected on his journey. He had built a strong financial foundation—his investments were compounding, his expenses were in check, and his emergency fund ensured peace of mind. Yet, he knew that true financial mastery was not just about numbers—it was about mindset.

That evening, he sat with Eshwar at their usual café.

Eshwar leaned in and asked, "Arjun, what do you think is the biggest difference between the wealthy and the struggling?"

Arjun thought for a moment and replied, **"Discipline, smart investing, and financial education."**

Eshwar nodded, then added, **"And their mindset. Your thoughts about money shape your financial future."**

The Scarcity vs. Abundance Mindset

Eshwar pulled out a napkin and wrote down two words:

- **Scarcity**
- **Abundance**

"Most people operate with a Scarcity Mindset," Eshwar explained.

"They believe that money is limited, opportunities are rare, and financial success is only for a lucky few."

Characteristics of a Scarcity Mindset:

- Fear of losing money—leading to excessive saving but no investing.
- Hesitation to take calculated risks—missing out on opportunities.
- Viewing others' success as a threat—competing instead of learning.
- Always worrying—never feeling 'secure' even with enough wealth.

Arjun nodded. "I've seen this in many people. Even high-income earners sometimes act like they're one step away from financial ruin."

Eshwar smiled. "Exactly! Now, let's talk about the Abundance Mindset."

"People with an Abundance Mindset see money as a tool, not a limitation. They believe wealth is created, not distributed. They don't hoard money—they make it work for them."

Characteristics of an Abundance Mindset:

- Seeing money as a means to grow, not just to survive.
- Taking calculated risks—investing instead of hoarding.
- Viewing failures as lessons, not roadblocks.
- Believing in continuous learning and wealth creation.

Arjun grinned. "That's how I think about money. I see it as a game of strategy, where knowledge and discipline lead to success."

Eshwar clapped him on the shoulder. "That's why you're on the right path, Arjun. The moment you shift from scarcity to abundance, your financial journey transforms."

Building a Wealth-Oriented Mindset

As their conversation continued, Arjun leaned forward, intrigued. **"So, how does one cultivate an abundance mindset?"**

Eshwar smiled. **"You already have it, Arjun. But for many people, it requires conscious effort to shift from a scarcity-driven outlook to a growth-oriented one."**

He outlined three key principles:

1. Investing Over Hoarding

Eshwar took a sip of his coffee and said, **"Most people think saving money is enough. But true wealth is built by making your money work for you."**

Arjun nodded. **"That's why I focus on investments. I don't let my money sit idle in a savings account. I ensure every rupee is either compounding in stocks, mutual funds, or other assets."**

Eshwar grinned. **"Exactly. The scarcity mindset makes people hoard cash because they fear losing it. The abundance mindset makes people invest because they know money grows when put to work."**

- **Scarcity Thinking**: "I need to save as much as possible to feel secure."
- **Abundance Thinking**: "I need to invest wisely to create financial freedom."

2. Viewing Failures as Lessons, Not Setbacks

Eshwar continued, **"Another key difference is how people handle failure. A scarcity mindset makes people afraid to take any risk, fearing loss. But successful investors understand that setbacks are part of the game."**

Arjun reflected on his past experiences. **"I've had investments that didn't perform well, but each one taught me something. I never see losses as failures—just as** learning experiences."

Eshwar nodded. "That's the right approach. Instead of fearing mistakes, those with an abundance mindset ask: 'What can I learn from this?'"

- **Scarcity Thinking**: "If I lose money, I'll never recover."
- **Abundance Thinking**: "Every experience—win or lose—teaches me something valuable."

3. Focusing on Growth, Not Just Security

Eshwar leaned back in his chair. "People with a scarcity mindset chase job security and avoid any financial risk. Those with an abundance mindset look for ways to grow—through skills, investments, and new opportunities."

Arjun smiled. "That's why I always reinvest a portion of my income into learning—whether it's books, courses, or experiences."

Eshwar raised his cup in approval. "That's how you stay ahead. When you focus on growth instead of just 'playing it safe,' you unlock true wealth creation."

- **Scarcity Thinking**: "I just need a stable job and a bank balance to feel safe."
- **Abundance Thinking**: "I need to keep learning, investing, and growing my financial knowledge."

CHAPTER FIFTEEN

Retiring Early & Financial Independence

The Real Meaning of Financial Independence

The office cafeteria buzzed with lunchtime chatter. Colleagues sat in small groups, exchanging stories about work, family, and weekend plans. Arjun absentmindedly stirred his tea, his mind lost in thought after an unexpected revelation.

"Did you hear about Ramesh?" a voice floated over from the next table.

"Yeah, he's retiring next month! Can you believe it?" another colleague responded, disbelief evident in his tone.

Arjun's ears perked up. *Ramesh? Retiring?*

He turned towards the conversation, listening closely.

"How is he retiring so early?" someone asked.

"Smart investing, I guess," replied another. "He planned it all in advance, saved aggressively, invested wisely, and now—he's free."

Arjun sat frozen. Ramesh was just 45. How could he already be at the finish line while Arjun felt like he was still running the race?

That evening, as Arjun stepped into his home, the question still lingered in his mind. He dropped his laptop bag on the couch and found Suneetha preparing dinner in the kitchen.

"Suneetha, guess what?" he said, sitting on a stool near the counter.

She glanced at him. "What happened?"

"Ramesh from my office... he's retiring next month."

She turned off the stove and gave him a puzzled look. "Retiring? He's hardly older than you, right?"

"Exactly!" Arjun leaned forward. "He's 45, and he's done. No more work. He's financially independent!"

Suneetha's eyebrows furrowed. "He must have inherited money or hit a jackpot in the stock market."

Arjun shook his head. "No inheritance, no lottery. Just planned investments and savings."

Suneetha let out a small laugh. "That sounds impossible. How can someone retire without having at least 10-15 crores?"

Arjun sighed. "That's exactly what I thought. I always assumed early retirement meant accumulating a massive fortune. But now I wonder... am I thinking about financial independence all wrong?"

That night, as Arjun lay in bed, staring at the ceiling, his mind refused to settle. Was he destined to work for another 20 years? Did he really have to wait until his 60s to enjoy true freedom?

The next morning, Arjun called Eshwar, his mentor, and asked if they could meet for coffee.

An hour later, they sat at their favorite café, a quiet place tucked away in the city's bustling streets.

Arjun wasted no time. "Eshwar, I need to ask you something. How do people retire early? I always thought you needed a huge bank balance to even consider it."

Eshwar smiled, taking a slow sip of his coffee. "That's the common misconception, Arjun. Most people assume financial independence is about hoarding wealth. But it's not about quitting work—it's about having the **freedom to choose how you live.**"

Arjun frowned. "Freedom? You mean, the freedom to not work?"

Eshwar set his cup down. "No, not exactly. Let me ask you something—if money were no longer a concern, would you still work?"

Arjun thought for a moment. "I think I would... but only on things I love. Maybe I'd teach investing, write about finance, or travel more."

Eshwar nodded. "That's exactly the point. Financial Independence is about removing the pressure of working for survival. It's about reaching a place where your **money works for you, instead of you working for money.**"

Arjun sat back, absorbing those words.

"So, it's not about a number in the bank, but about reaching a point where my investments can cover my lifestyle?"

"Exactly," Eshwar said. "Retirement doesn't mean sitting idle. It means **having the choice** to work or not. To spend time the way you want, without financial stress dictating your decisions."

Arjun took a deep breath. For the first time, he saw **financial independence not as an endpoint, but as a gateway to freedom.**

That night, as he drove home, his mind was racing. He had always thought financial independence was a distant dream, something only the ultra-rich could achieve. But now, he realized—**maybe it was within his reach, too.**

The FIRE Movement: Can You Retire Early?

Arjun sat at his desk, but his mind was elsewhere. The words from his conversation with Eshwar kept playing in his head.

"It's not about quitting work, it's about having the choice to live on your terms."

But how? How could someone actually reach that level of financial freedom?

Determined to find out, he spent his lunch break researching online. That's when he stumbled upon a term he had never heard before—**FIRE**: *Financial Independence, Retire Early.*

The idea fascinated him. People retiring in their 40s, some even in their 30s? It seemed unbelievable. Yet, here were real stories—engineers, teachers, even middle-class employees—who had achieved it.

That evening, he met Eshwar again. As soon as they sat down, Arjun leaned forward eagerly.

"Eshwar, have you heard about the FIRE movement?"

Eshwar smiled knowingly. "Of course. It's a financial philosophy that's changing the way people think about money."

Arjun's excitement grew. "I read that some people save almost 70% of their income to retire in their 40s! But how is that even possible?"

Eshwar leaned back, his expression thoughtful. "There isn't just one way to achieve FIRE. There are different paths, depending on how much you want to save and what kind of lifestyle you want after retirement."

He picked up a tissue and scribbled three words on it:

Lean FIRE. Fat FIRE. Coast FIRE.

Arjun raised an eyebrow. "What do these mean?"

1. Lean FIRE – The Frugal Path

Eshwar pointed at the first term. "Lean FIRE is for people who focus on extreme frugality. They minimize expenses, live very simply, and save aggressively to retire early."

Arjun frowned. "So, they just live like misers?"

Eshwar chuckled. "Not necessarily. They prioritize what matters. No luxury cars, no expensive vacations, no eating out every weekend. They invest almost everything they earn so that they can achieve financial independence as fast as possible."

Arjun nodded slowly. "That sounds... challenging. But doable."

2. Fat FIRE – The Luxury Retirement

Eshwar tapped the next term. "Fat FIRE is the opposite. This is for those who don't want to compromise on lifestyle. They still aim to retire early, but they build a larger investment portfolio to sustain a comfortable or even luxurious life."

Arjun smirked. "So, these are the people who still want their foreign vacations and five-star dining?"

"Exactly," Eshwar said. "They don't just want to survive—they want to enjoy."

Arjun thought about it. He liked the idea of retiring early, but he didn't want to live a restricted life. **Could he aim for Fat FIRE instead of Lean FIRE?**

3. Coast FIRE – The Slow & Steady Approach

Finally, Eshwar pointed to the last term. "Coast FIRE is a hybrid model. You invest heavily in the early years, and then let compounding do the rest. After a point, you don't have to save aggressively anymore—your investments will grow on their own to fund your retirement."

Arjun's eyes widened. "That sounds more practical! You mean, I don't have to save 50-70% of my income forever?"

"Exactly," Eshwar said. "For example, if you invest heavily in your 20s and 30s, by the time you're in your 40s, you might not need to save much at all. Your investments will grow enough to support you later."

How FIRE Could Work for Arjun

Arjun took a deep breath. "So, if I start now, how soon can I reach financial independence?"

Eshwar grabbed a pen and jotted down some numbers.

"Let's say you invest   ₹50,000 per month in equity mutual funds. Assuming an average return of 12% per year, you could build a   ₹5 crore corpus in 15-20 years."

Arjun stared at the number.   **₹5 crore.**

With that kind of money, he wouldn't have to work for a salary. He could spend his time however he wanted.

"But is it practical?" Arjun asked. "I have a family. Expenses will keep increasing. What if I can't save that much?"

Eshwar nodded. "That's why FIRE is flexible. You can adjust the path based on your savings rate and investment strategy. The key is consistency."

Arjun leaned back, his mind racing with possibilities. **For the first time, early retirement didn't feel like an impossible dream.**

It was just a matter of choosing the right approach and sticking to it.

The Key to Early Retirement: The Savings Rate

The next morning, Arjun sat at his usual corner in the office cafeteria, lost in thought. The conversation with Eshwar the previous evening had ignited something inside him. **Financial Independence was no longer just an abstract idea—it felt like a real possibility.**

But one question kept nagging him.

"How much should I be saving?"

As if on cue, his phone buzzed. It was Eshwar.

"Let's meet for coffee today. I have something important to show you."

Later that evening, they sat in their favorite café. Arjun wasted no time.

"Eshwar, I've been thinking a lot about FIRE. I understand the different approaches, but how do I figure out how much I should save? Is there a fixed number?"

Eshwar smiled. "There's no single number, Arjun. But there *is* a simple formula that will tell you exactly how soon you can retire."

He took a tissue and started writing:

Years to Retirement = (Wealth Target - Current Savings) / Annual Savings

Arjun leaned in. "So, the more I save, the faster I can retire?"

"Exactly," Eshwar nodded. "Your savings rate—how much of your income you save and invest—matters more than how much you earn."

Arjun frowned. "But isn't earning more also important?"

"Of course," Eshwar said. "But most people don't realize this—**even if you earn ₹10 lakh a month, if you spend ₹10 lakh a month, you'll never retire.** On the other hand, someone earning ₹1 lakh a month but saving 50% of it will achieve financial independence much faster."

Arjun thought about it. He knew people who made fortunes yet always complained about money. **And he had also met simple, middle-class people who retired peacefully.**

"So, what's the ideal savings rate?" he asked.

Eshwar grinned. "Let me show you something interesting."

He pulled out his phone and opened a chart.

How Your Savings Rate Affects Retirement

- Saving 10% of income → Retire in 51 years
- Saving 20% of income → Retire in 36 years
- Saving 30% of income → Retire in 28 years
- Saving 50% of income → Retire in 15 years
- Saving 70% of income → Retire in 8 years

Arjun's jaw dropped. "Wait, if I save 50% of my income, I can retire in just 15 years?!"

Eshwar nodded. "That's the power of savings. Every rupee you save today buys you *time* in the future."

Arjun sat back, stunned. He had always thought of savings as a boring, tedious task. But now, he saw it differently. **Every extra rupee saved was a step closer to freedom.**

"But wait," Arjun said, "isn't saving 50% of income unrealistic?"

Eshwar smiled. "It depends on priorities. Look at your expenses. **How much do you spend on things that truly make you happy? And how much is just impulse or social pressure?**"

Arjun's mind flashed back to his past spending habits—fancy gadgets, expensive clothes, dining out at lavish restaurants, all for the sake of *status*.

How many of those things had genuinely improved his life?

Not many.

The Realization

For the first time, Arjun saw **money not as something to spend, but as a tool to buy freedom.**

He pulled out his notepad and started making calculations.

- If he increased his savings from 20% to 40%, he could retire **10 years earlier.**
- If he saved 50%, he could retire **even before 50.**
- If he followed the *Coast FIRE* strategy, he could front-load investments in the next 10 years and let compounding do the rest.

He looked up at Eshwar, his eyes shining with excitement.

"I always thought financial independence was for the super-rich. But it's just a numbers game, isn't it?"

Eshwar chuckled. "Exactly. **It's not about how much you earn. It's about how much you keep and grow.**"

Arjun had always been disciplined with money, but today, something had shifted inside him.

This wasn't just about saving. **This was about buying back his life.**

The 4% Rule: How Much Do You Need to Retire?

The next evening, Arjun sat in his study, deep in thought.

For the past 24 hours, he had been obsessing over his savings rate. He had already started analyzing his expenses, identifying unnecessary costs, and making a plan to increase his savings.

But one question remained unanswered—**how much money did he actually need to retire?**

He dialed Eshwar's number.

"Eshwar, I've figured out how to save more, but how do I know when I've saved *enough*?"

Eshwar laughed. "That's the million-dollar question, isn't it? Let's meet and break it down."

The Magic Number for Retirement

When they met later that evening, Eshwar handed Arjun a notepad.

"There's a simple formula," he said, writing down:

Annual Expenses × 25 = Retirement Corpus

Arjun frowned. "Why 25?"

"This is based on the **4% Rule**," Eshwar explained. "It's a strategy that says if you withdraw only 4% of your portfolio every year, your money should last forever."

He leaned forward. "Think about it. If your annual expenses are ₹10 lakh, you need ₹2.5 crore to retire. That way, withdrawing 4% every year gives you ₹10 lakh without ever running out of money."

Arjun's eyes widened. "That sounds too simple to be true."

Eshwar smiled. "It's based on historical data from the stock market. Over the last century, a well-diversified portfolio of stocks and bonds has returned more than 7% per year on average. Even after adjusting for inflation, withdrawing 4% keeps your portfolio growing."

Arjun's mind started racing.

He quickly did some calculations.

- If he needed ₹12 lakh a year to sustain his current lifestyle, he would need ₹3 crore.
- If he reduced his annual expenses to ₹8 lakh, he could retire with ₹2 crore.
- If he invested wisely, he could reach this number faster.

He looked up. "So, financial independence isn't about having *crores* of rupees. It's just about covering my expenses from my investments?"

"Exactly!" Eshwar said. **"The lower your expenses, the faster you can reach financial freedom."**

Adjusting for India: The Inflation Challenge

Arjun nodded, but a thought struck him.

"Wait, India has higher inflation than the US. Won't the 4% rule fail here?"

Eshwar smiled. "Good question. You're right—our inflation is usually higher. That's why, in India, we can't rely only on fixed deposits or bonds. We need a mix of:

- **Equities** (for long-term growth)
- **Fixed-income assets** (for stability)
- **Real estate** (for rental income, if possible)"

He continued, "If your portfolio grows at 12% and inflation is 6%, your real return is still 6%. That means the 4% rule still works if your money is invested wisely."

Arjun thought about his own investments. **So far, he had focused on savings, but now he realized that *where* he invested mattered just as much as *how much* he saved.**

"So, I should aim to build a ₹3 crore portfolio invested in growth assets, withdraw only 4% per year, and I'm financially free?"

"Precisely," Eshwar said. "And if you earn any passive income along the way—like rental income, dividends, or side projects—you can retire even earlier."

Arjun smiled. **For the first time, financial freedom felt within reach.**

Breaking Free from the Salary Trap

That night, Arjun lay in bed staring at the ceiling.

For years, he had believed that financial security meant having a **high-paying job** and **climbing the corporate ladder**. But today's discussion with Eshwar had **changed everything**.

He now realized something shocking—**even people earning   ₹1 crore per year can be financially trapped if they spend everything they earn.**

The real path to freedom wasn't about **earning more**. It was about **owning assets that paid for his expenses**.

Arjun suddenly sat up. He needed to talk to Eshwar again.

"But What If I Need More Money?"

The next morning, Arjun and Eshwar met again over coffee.

"I get the 4% rule," Arjun said, "but what if I'm wrong about my expenses? What if I need more money later? What if unexpected medical bills come up? What if my kids want to study abroad?"

Eshwar smiled. "That's why financial independence isn't just about saving a big lump sum. It's also about building **multiple income streams**."

Arjun raised an eyebrow. "Multiple streams?"

Eshwar nodded. "Think about it this way. Instead of **just saving a retirement corpus**, you should also build **passive income sources** like:

- **Dividends from stocks**
- **Rental income from real estate**
- **Interest from bonds and deposits**
- **Side businesses or royalties**

"That way," Eshwar continued, "even if your expenses increase in the future, you won't have to panic. Your passive income will keep flowing."

Arjun's mind started racing. **He always thought of retirement as "one big savings account," but now he saw it differently.**

Instead of relying only on a retirement fund, he could **set up systems that paid him forever.**

The Transition to Freedom

"So," Arjun said, "if I want to retire early, I need three things—"

He held up his fingers and counted:

1. **A strong investment portfolio** (stocks, mutual funds, real estate, and fixed income)
2. **A low cost of living** (or at least controlled expenses)
3. **Reliable passive income streams**

Eshwar smiled. "Exactly. Most people only focus on one—saving a big corpus. But if you build assets that generate income, you'll never have to worry about running out of money."

Arjun nodded slowly.

He had always thought **financial freedom meant quitting work completely.**

But now, he saw it differently—it **meant having the choice to work on his own terms.**

For the first time, retirement didn't feel like a distant dream. It felt **possible.**

"Can I Really Do This?" – Overcoming the Fear of Early Retirement

Even though everything Eshwar said made sense, a tiny voice in Arjun's mind whispered doubts.

What if I miscalculate?

What if I run out of money at 60?

What if something unexpected happens?

The fear of stepping away from the security of a **monthly salary** was real.

"Eshwar," Arjun said hesitantly, "all of this sounds amazing. But what if something goes wrong? What if I retire early and later regret it?"

Eshwar leaned back in his chair. "That's a natural fear, Arjun. Society has trained us to believe that a job is the safest way to survive. But let me ask you something—"

He looked directly at Arjun. "If you **lost your job tomorrow**, what would you do?"

Arjun blinked. "I'd... find another job, I guess."

"And what if no company hired you?"

Arjun frowned. "I'd figure something out... Maybe start consulting, invest more aggressively, or build another income source."

Eshwar smiled. "Exactly. You'd **find a way**. The problem isn't retirement—it's the **fear of the unknown**. But you already have the skills, the knowledge, and the mindset to adapt."

Arjun took a deep breath. He had never thought about it that way.

People feared retirement because they imagined **a life without income**. But in reality, early retirees weren't "stopping" work—they were **working in ways they enjoyed, without financial pressure**.

Taking the First Step Toward Financial Independence

"So, how do I start?" Arjun asked.

Eshwar's answer was simple:

- **Calculate your "FI Number"** – The amount you need to live comfortably for life.

- **Increase your savings rate** – The more you save, the sooner you retire.
- **Invest in assets that generate income** – Stocks, bonds, real estate, or businesses.
- **Test financial independence before quitting** – Live off investments for a year while still working.

Arjun felt a surge of confidence.

He didn't need to retire tomorrow. But if he followed this plan, he could **become financially independent** within the next decade.

And that meant something even more powerful than retiring early—**the ability to live life on his own terms.**

Avoiding Common Pitfalls in Early Retirement

Arjun sat in his balcony, sipping his evening coffee, staring at the horizon where the sun was setting. The idea of early retirement fascinated him. The thought of having the freedom to wake up whenever he wanted, travel, or even pursue a passion without worrying about money seemed like the ultimate dream.

But something nagged at him. He had read stories of people who retired early only to find themselves struggling a few years later. How did that happen? Weren't they supposed to be financially independent?

Sensing Arjun's dilemma, Eshwar leaned forward with a knowing smile. "Arjun, financial independence is only half the battle. The real challenge is sustaining it."

1. Underestimating Expenses

"Many people calculate their retirement needs based on their current lifestyle," Eshwar began, "but what they forget is that life doesn't remain constant."

He picked up a small pebble and tossed it into the garden. "Think about it—medical expenses rise as you age, inflation eats into your purchasing power, and unexpected emergencies always pop up."

Arjun nodded. He had seen retirees in his own family struggle with rising healthcare costs. "So, what's the solution?" he asked.

"You need to **overestimate your expenses, not underestimate them**," Eshwar said. "Most people assume their expenses will go down after retirement, but that's rarely the case. Travel, hobbies, home renovations—these things cost money. You must prepare for them."

Arjun mentally noted to revisit his retirement calculations.

2. Over-Reliance on One Income Source

"Another big mistake," Eshwar continued, "is depending on just one source of income after retirement."

Arjun thought for a moment. "You mean, like relying only on rental income or dividends?"

"Exactly," Eshwar confirmed. "What if your rental property remains vacant for a year? What if dividends are cut during a market crash? You need multiple income streams—investments, pensions, part-time work, or even a small side business. That way, if one source falters, you're still financially secure."

This made perfect sense to Arjun. He had always assumed a solid corpus was enough, but diversifying income streams could act as a safety net.

3. Ignoring Inflation and Withdrawal Rates

"Many people think they need, say, ₹2 crores to retire early. But what they don't realize is that inflation can eat away at that money faster than they expect."

Eshwar leaned back and sipped his tea. "Let's assume your monthly expenses today are ₹50,000. In 20 years, even at a modest 6% inflation rate, they'll be around ₹

1.6 lakh. If you haven't accounted for that, your financial independence will be short-lived."

Arjun's eyes widened. "That's a scary thought."

"That's why the **withdrawal rate** is crucial," Eshwar explained. "The 4% rule is a general guideline, but in India, it's safer to start with a lower withdrawal rate—around 3.5%—to ensure your money lasts longer."

4. Not Having a Plan for Purpose and Engagement

Arjun frowned. "But what about the emotional side of early retirement? Some people say they feel lost after quitting their job."

Eshwar smiled. "You're absolutely right. Many people assume retirement means **sitting on a beach, sipping coconut water forever.** But after a few months, they start feeling restless, even depressed. Humans need purpose. Without meaningful activities, early retirees can struggle with boredom, lack of identity, or even a sense of uselessness."

Arjun nodded slowly. "So, what's the solution?"

"Before you retire, plan for how you'll **spend your time productively.** Whether it's consulting, teaching, traveling, or volunteering—keep yourself engaged. Financial freedom is about choice, not just money."

Arjun let the words sink in. Financial independence wasn't just about accumulating wealth—it was about **sustaining it wisely, planning for risks, and ensuring life remained fulfilling.**

He smiled. "I think I'm getting a clearer picture now."

Eshwar chuckled. "Good. Because retirement isn't about stopping—it's about having the freedom to do what truly matters to you."

How to Stay Financially Secure After Retiring – Managing Money After Achieving Financial

Independence

The idea of early retirement excited Arjun, but a nagging question lingered in his mind.

"Eshwar, let's assume I reach financial independence and retire early. But what happens after that? How do I make sure my money lasts for the rest of my life?"

Eshwar nodded knowingly. "Ah, that's the part most people don't think about. Achieving financial independence is just half the journey; managing wealth wisely after retirement is just as important."

He took a deep breath and continued. "Retiring early doesn't mean you can just sit back and withdraw money randomly. If you don't manage your post-retirement finances properly, you could run out of money faster than you expect."

1. The Importance of Sustainable Withdrawals

Eshwar pulled out a napkin and began scribbling some numbers.

"There's a rule called the 4% rule. It suggests that if you withdraw 4% of your corpus annually, your money should last for at least 30 years. For example, if your retirement corpus is ₹3 crore, you can withdraw ₹ 12 lakh per year."

Arjun frowned. "But what if inflation increases? What if unexpected expenses arise?"

Eshwar smiled. "Exactly. That's why we can't blindly follow a single rule. The 4% rule was designed for the Western world, where inflation is lower. In India, where inflation is higher, we need a more flexible approach."

2. Creating Multiple Streams of Passive Income

"Arjun, the smartest way to stay financially secure after retirement is to not depend solely on one source of income. Even after retiring, your money should continue working for you."

Arjun leaned in with interest.

"Think about setting up multiple streams of passive income—rental income from real estate, dividends from stocks, interest from bonds, and even side income from hobbies you enjoy."

Arjun's eyes lit up. "So even though I'm retired, I should keep some investments active?"

Eshwar nodded. "Exactly! You don't want to touch your principal investment too soon. Instead, you should live off the returns your investments generate. If done correctly, you might not even need to withdraw from your retirement corpus for a long time."

3. Keeping a Cash Reserve for Emergencies

Arjun thought back to past financial crises—unexpected medical emergencies, sudden market crashes. "But what about emergencies? What if the market crashes and my investments lose value?"

Eshwar tapped the table. "That's why you always need a safety net. Keep at least two years' worth of expenses in a liquid, low-risk fund—something like a fixed deposit, a liquid mutual fund, or even a savings account. This ensures that you don't have to sell your investments during a market downturn."

Arjun nodded. "So instead of panicking and selling stocks at a loss, I can rely on my cash reserves."

Eshwar smiled. "Now you're thinking like a financially independent person."

4. Adjusting Your Spending to Market Conditions

Eshwar leaned in. "Here's another trick. You don't need to withdraw the same amount every year. If the market performs well, you can take out a little more. But if the market is down, reduce your spending slightly to allow your investments to recover."

Arjun nodded slowly. **"So financial independence isn't just about having a big corpus. It's also about managing it wisely after retirement."**

Eshwar beamed. **"Exactly! True financial independence is not just about quitting your job; it's about never worrying about money again."**

Arjun leaned back in his chair, deep in thought. For the first time, he truly understood that financial independence wasn't just about reaching a number—it was about making sure that number lasted for life.

Conclusion: The True Meaning of Financial Freedom

As Arjun sat back, absorbing everything Eshwar had explained, a deep sense of clarity settled within him. Financial independence was not just about accumulating wealth—it was about control, choices, and peace of mind.

He had always thought early retirement meant walking away from work forever. But now, he understood it was not about stopping work but about having the freedom to decide *how* to live. Some might continue working because they love what they do. Others might travel, pursue passions, or spend time with family. The key was not to escape work but to escape *the need* to work for survival.

Eshwar's final words echoed in his mind:

"True financial freedom isn't about how much money you have in the bank. It's about never having to make a decision based on financial fear. It's about waking up every morning knowing you have full control over your life."

Arjun smiled. He had started this journey thinking about wealth. Now, he realized the real goal was *freedom*. And that freedom was worth every step of discipline, every investment, and every smart financial decision he would make.

With a renewed sense of purpose, Arjun knew he wasn't just chasing money—he was building a life where money would never dictate his choices again.

CHAPTER SIXTEEN

Teaching Financial Literacy to the Next Generation

The Importance of Financial Education for Children

It was a bright Sunday morning, and Arjun was enjoying his coffee while watching his son, Aditya, excitedly count the crisp   ₹100 notes he had received as pocket money from relatives. His small hands carefully arranged them on the table, his face glowing with anticipation.

"Papa, can we go to the toy store today? I want that new remote-controlled car!" Aditya chirped, his eyes sparkling.

Arjun smiled. "You just got this money, beta. Why don't you save some of it?"

Aditya shook his head. "No! I want to buy something *now*! What's the point of saving?"

Arjun leaned back in his chair, his smile fading slightly. This was a pattern he had noticed before—whenever Aditya got money, he would spend it impulsively on toys, chocolates, or games, never thinking beyond the immediate thrill. It was a stark contrast to how Arjun handled money himself.

At that moment, a memory flashed through Arjun's mind—his own childhood. His parents had been careful with money, but they had never explicitly taught him how to manage it. He had learned through experience, sometimes through mistakes. *Would Aditya have to learn the hard way too?*

That evening, he shared his concern with Eshwar.

"You know, schools teach kids about history, science, and maths... but they never teach them about money," Arjun sighed. "I mean, when I was growing up, I had no clue about savings, investing, or even budgeting. I just watched my parents struggle and assumed that's how life is."

Eshwar nodded. "That's because financial education isn't considered a priority in schools. But money is a part of our lives every single day. If we don't teach our kids how to manage it, the world will teach them the wrong way."

Arjun thought for a moment. "But how do I start? He's just a child. He won't understand concepts like savings, investments, or inflation."

Eshwar chuckled. "You don't start with stock markets and mutual funds, Arjun. You start simple. Teach him what money is, where it comes from, and most importantly—how to respect it."

Arjun felt a deep sense of responsibility. *I work so hard to secure my family's future, but if I don't teach my kids how to handle money wisely, they might repeat the same mistakes many adults make.*

That night, he sat beside Aditya and asked, "Beta, do you know where money comes from?"

Aditya giggled, holding up a ₹100 note. "From your wallet!"

Arjun laughed but shook his head. "No, son. I earn money by working hard at my job. Money isn't just something that appears when you want it—it's something you have to earn and manage carefully."

Aditya looked curious. "But if you have money, why can't I buy whatever I want?"

Arjun smiled. "Because money isn't just for buying toys. It has to be used wisely—for food, our house, your school, and also for the future. If I spent all my money the way you spend yours, we wouldn't have a home to live in!"

Aditya's eyes widened. "Oh..."

For the first time, he seemed to be grasping that money wasn't just a magical tool for instant gratification.

That was the beginning of Arjun's journey in teaching his son financial literacy—not through lectures, but through real-life lessons, small conversations, and leading by example.

Understanding Money: The First Step

The next morning, Arjun decided to take a different approach. Instead of just telling Aditya about money, he wanted him to experience it firsthand.

At breakfast, he placed three different items on the table—a glass of milk, a toy car, and a packet of chips.

"Aditya, let's play a game," Arjun said, leaning forward with a smile. "Imagine you have ₹50. You can buy only two of these things. What will you choose?"

Aditya's eyes darted between the items. "Easy! The toy car and the chips!" he announced confidently.

Arjun chuckled. "Okay, but if you don't choose the milk, what will you drink with breakfast?"

Aditya frowned. "Umm... but I really want the toy car."

Arjun leaned in. "That's called a choice, beta. Money lets us buy things, but we can't buy everything we want. We have to decide between needs and wants. Milk is a *need* because it keeps you healthy. A toy car is a *want* because it's something fun but not necessary. If we spend all our money on wants, we might not have enough for our needs."

Aditya looked at the items again, his tiny fingers tapping his chin. "So... money is not just for spending?"

Arjun smiled. "Exactly! Money is a tool. If you use it wisely, it helps you get what you need and also enjoy what you want. But if you waste it, you might struggle later."

That afternoon, Arjun met Eshwar at the park and shared what had happened.

Eshwar nodded approvingly. "That's a great start. Kids understand best through examples. Keep doing this in everyday life."

"But how do I take it further?" Arjun asked.

Eshwar tapped his walking stick on the ground thoughtfully. "Start by explaining where money comes from. Kids think money is unlimited because they see parents swiping cards or withdrawing cash from ATMs. They don't realize that money has to be earned."

That evening, Arjun sat with Aditya and asked, "Do you know how I get money?"

Aditya grinned. "From your office?"

"Yes, but I don't just *get* money. I *earn* it by working hard. Every month, my company pays me because I use my time and skills to help them. If I don't work, I won't earn money."

Aditya's eyes widened. "So money doesn't just come from ATMs?"

Arjun laughed. "No, beta. An ATM is like a water tank. You can only take out water if you fill the tank first. If I don't earn money and put it in the bank, I won't be able to withdraw anything."

Aditya was silent for a moment. Then he asked, "So I should also earn money?"

Arjun smiled. "Not yet. But you should learn how to use money wisely. Let's start by keeping track of what you spend. Every time you buy something, write it down. Then, at the end of the week, we'll see where your money is going."

Excited by the idea, Aditya grabbed a notebook and titled it "My Money." He had just taken his first step toward financial awareness, and Arjun felt proud.

Introducing the Concept of Saving

A few days after their conversation about money, Arjun decided it was time for Aditya to learn about saving.

That evening, he sat down with his son and placed a shiny new piggy bank on the table.

Aditya's eyes lit up. "What's this, Papa?"

"This," Arjun said, tapping the piggy bank, "is your new money vault. From now on, every time you get pocket money or someone gives you a gift in cash, you'll put some of it in here. It's called *saving*."

Aditya wrinkled his nose. "But why should I keep money here? I can just buy chocolates and toys right away!"

Arjun smiled. "That's exactly what most people do. But let me tell you a little secret—rich people don't just spend all their money. They save first and spend later."

Aditya looked intrigued. "How does that help?"

Arjun picked up a ₹10 coin and held it between his fingers. "Let's say you get ₹100 as pocket money. If you spend everything on chocolates, it's gone. But if you save ₹50 and spend only ₹50, you'll still have money left for something bigger later. Imagine you want a cricket bat that costs ₹500. If you save a little every time, you'll be able to buy it yourself!"

Aditya's eyes widened. "Really? I can buy my own cricket bat?"

"Absolutely! And it will feel much better because you earned it by saving," Arjun said.

Aditya grinned and dropped the first ₹10 into the piggy bank with a satisfying *clink*.

Later that night, Arjun shared this small victory with Eshwar.

"That's a great start," Eshwar said. "Now, let's make it even more fun. Introduce him to the *three-jar method*."

"The three-jar method?" Arjun asked.

"Yes," Eshwar nodded. "It's a simple system for kids. Get three jars and label them: *Spend*, *Save*, and *Give*. Every time Aditya gets money, he divides it among the three jars."

Arjun was curious. "How does it help?"

"The *Spend Jar* is for small treats, like chocolates or toys. The *Save Jar* is for bigger things, like the cricket bat. And the *Give Jar* is for helping others—maybe donating to a charity or buying something for someone in need."

Arjun loved the idea and introduced it to Aditya the next day.

"From now on," Arjun explained, "whenever you get money, you'll put some in each jar."

Aditya eagerly set up the three jars, labeling them with his own handwriting.

For the first time, he felt like he was in control of his money. Instead of spending everything on instant treats, he started looking forward to filling up his Save Jar.

One evening, a few weeks later, Aditya held up his jar proudly. "Papa! I have ₹300 now! That means I'm getting closer to my cricket bat!"

Arjun beamed with pride. "Yes, beta! And do you see how saving a little at a time adds up?"

Aditya nodded enthusiastically. "Yes! I'm going to keep saving more!"

Arjun knew then that this small lesson would stay with his son for life. He was not just teaching him to save—he was teaching him patience, discipline, and the value of money.

Earning Money: Teaching Kids the Value of Hard Work

A few weeks after introducing the three-jar method, Arjun noticed something.

Aditya was diligently putting money into his *Save Jar*, but he seemed frustrated.

One evening, as they sat in the living room, Aditya sighed. "Papa, saving takes so long. I still don't have enough for my cricket bat."

Arjun chuckled. "That's true, beta. But do you know there's a way to speed it up?"

Aditya's eyes lit up. "Really? How?"

"By earning money."

Aditya frowned. "But I'm just a kid. How can I earn money?"

Arjun leaned forward. "Earning money isn't about age. It's about effort. If you do something useful, people will pay for it. Even small tasks can help you earn."

Aditya looked interested. "Like what?"

Arjun thought for a moment. "How about this? I'll give you small tasks around the house, and for every task you complete well, I'll give you a small reward."

Aditya grinned. "Like a job?"

"Exactly!" Arjun said. "But not for things you should already be doing—like your homework or keeping your room clean. These will be extra tasks that add value."

The next morning, Arjun handed Aditya a small list:

- Watering the plants every evening – ₹10 per week
- Arranging bookshelves neatly – ₹5 per week
- Washing the car with me on Sundays – ₹20 per week

Aditya's eyes sparkled. "This is awesome! I'm going to be rich!"

Arjun laughed. "Not rich, but you'll reach your goal faster."

Over the next few weeks, Aditya enthusiastically completed his tasks. He watered the plants, organized books, and scrubbed the car with great energy. Every Sunday, Arjun paid him and watched as Aditya excitedly dropped his earnings into the *Save Jar*.

One day, as they were cleaning the car together, Aditya asked, "Papa, do grown-ups earn money like this too?"

Arjun smiled. "Yes, beta. But the world works a little differently. Adults earn by using their skills—some are doctors, engineers, teachers. The harder they work and the more valuable their skills, the more they earn."

Aditya thought for a moment. "So, if I study well and learn new things, I can earn more when I grow up?"

Arjun nodded. "Exactly. The better your skills, the more valuable you become. And just like now, if you save and invest wisely, you'll never have to worry about money."

A month later, Aditya ran to Arjun, holding up his Save Jar proudly. "Papa! I did it! I saved ₹500! I can buy my cricket bat now!"

Arjun hugged him. "I'm proud of you, Aditya. You didn't just get a cricket bat—you learned how to earn and manage money."

That evening, when they went to the store, Arjun let Aditya pay for the bat himself. As he handed over the money, Aditya beamed with pride.

For the first time, he understood the joy of earning something through hard work.

Arjun watched his son with pride. This wasn't just about a cricket bat. It was about teaching him self-reliance—one of the most important money lessons of all.

The First Bank Account & Investing Basics

A few weeks after Aditya bought his cricket bat, Arjun noticed something interesting.

Aditya had continued doing his chores, but this time, he wasn't spending all his earnings. Instead, he was still dropping money into his *Save Jar*.

One evening, Arjun asked, "Aditya, you already bought your cricket bat. Why are you still saving?"

Aditya grinned. "I don't know, Papa. It just feels good to see my money grow."

Arjun's heart swelled with pride. His son was already learning an important lesson—saving wasn't just about buying things; it was about financial security and growth.

Smiling, he ruffled Aditya's hair. "If you like watching your money grow, I think it's time for the next step."

Aditya's eyes widened. "Next step?"

"Yes," Arjun said. "It's time to open your very own bank account."

A Visit to the Bank

The next weekend, Arjun took Aditya to the bank. As they stepped inside, Aditya looked around curiously at the counters, the people filling forms, and the cashiers counting money.

"What happens here, Papa?" he asked.

"This is where people keep their money safely," Arjun explained. "Banks help us store, save, and even grow our money."

They approached the customer service desk. The banker smiled at Aditya and said, "So, young man, are you ready to open your first savings account?"

Aditya nodded eagerly. Arjun helped him fill out the forms, and soon, Aditya had his own minor savings account.

The banker handed him a small passbook. "This will keep track of your money. Whenever you deposit or withdraw, it will be recorded here."

Aditya held the passbook like it was a treasure map. "So I can put my money here instead of my Save Jar?"

"Yes," Arjun said. "And the best part? The bank will *add* a little extra money to your savings every few months. It's called *interest*."

Aditya's eyes widened. "The bank gives me extra money just for keeping my savings here?"

Arjun laughed. "Yes! That's why saving in a bank is better than keeping cash at home."

As they left the bank, Aditya clutched his passbook proudly. He felt like a grown-up managing real money.

The Magic of Investing

That evening, as they sat down for dinner, Aditya asked, "Papa, if saving in a bank helps my money grow a little, is there a way to make it grow *a lot*?"

Arjun smiled. "Yes. That's called *investing*."

"Investing?" Aditya frowned. "What's that?"

Arjun took out his phone and opened a stock market app. "See this? These are companies. When you invest in them, you become a part-owner."

Aditya gasped. "Part-owner? Like I own a company?"

"Exactly," Arjun said. "When these companies grow, your investment grows too."

He paused for a moment. "Tell me, which company made your favorite chocolate?"

"Cadbury!" Aditya said instantly.

"Well," Arjun said, "If you invest in Cadbury's parent company, every time people buy their chocolates, you make a little money too."

Aditya's jaw dropped. "That's amazing! Can I invest in chocolates?"

Arjun chuckled. "Yes, but it's better to invest in a mix of things. Some in chocolates, some in banks, some in tech companies."

Then, he did something unexpected. He opened his investing app, bought one share of a well-known company, and transferred it to Aditya's account.

"This is your first investment," Arjun said. "Over time, you'll see how it grows."

Aditya was speechless. He wasn't just a kid saving money anymore—he was an *investor*.

That night, as he went to bed, Aditya hugged his passbook and whispered, "I own a company."

Arjun smiled. His son had taken the first step toward financial independence—years ahead of most people.

Budgeting for Kids: Learning to Make Choices

A few weeks after opening his bank account, Aditya's excitement about saving and investing was still strong. Every time he earned some money, he carefully decided how much to spend and how much to save.

One evening, as Arjun returned home from work, he saw Aditya sitting at the dining table with a notebook, staring at his three jars—Spend, Save, and Give.

"What's up, champ?" Arjun asked, setting down his laptop bag.

Aditya sighed. "Papa, I want to buy a remote-controlled car, but I also want to save more money in my bank account. And I don't know how much to put in the Give Jar either."

Arjun smiled. "Sounds like you're facing your first real money decision. Let me teach you something that will help—*budgeting*."

"Budgeting?" Aditya tilted his head. "What's that?"

"It's like making a plan for your money before you spend it," Arjun explained. "Think of it as making a shopping list before going to the store, so you don't waste money on things you don't really need."

Aditya nodded slowly. "Okay... how do I do it?"

Arjun grabbed a notebook and drew three columns:

1. **Income (Money coming in)**
2. **Expenses (Money going out)**
3. **Savings (Money kept for the future)**

"First, we write down how much money you have right now."

Aditya quickly added up his pocket money, the money he earned from small chores, and the occasional gifts from relatives. "I have ₹1,500 in total."

"Great," Arjun said. "Now, let's plan how to use it wisely."

The Budgeting Process Begins

Arjun continued, "Now, let's break your money into three categories: Spending, Saving, and Giving. You should decide how much goes where."

Aditya thought for a moment and said, "I need at least ₹1,000 for the remote-controlled car."

Arjun nodded. "That means you'll have ₹500 left. How much do you want to save?"

Aditya looked at his Save Jar and thought about his bank account. "I think I should save ₹300."

"Good choice," Arjun said. "That leaves ₹200. Do you want to donate some to the Give Jar?"

Aditya hesitated, then nodded. "I'll put ₹100 in the Give Jar. The last ₹100 I'll keep in my Spend Jar for small things, like chocolates or stickers."

Arjun wrote it all down in the notebook and showed Aditya:

Aditya's Budget for the Month:

- **Income:** ₹1,500
- **Expenses:**

  - Remote-controlled car: ₹1,000
  - Small spending: ₹100

- **Savings:** ₹300
- **Giving:** ₹100

Aditya's face lit up. "Wow, this actually makes sense! I can get my car *and* still save money!"

Arjun smiled. "Exactly! A budget helps you control your money instead of your money controlling you."

The Lesson of Delayed Gratification

A few days later, Aditya was about to buy his remote-controlled car when he saw a bigger, fancier model at the toy store. It had more features, bigger wheels, and even lights!

He turned to Arjun. "Papa, I want *this* one instead!"

Arjun checked the price. "But this one costs ₹1,800. You only have ₹1,000 in your budget."

Aditya's excitement faded. "Oh... so I can't buy it?"

Arjun smiled and asked, "What do you *think* you can do?"

Aditya thought hard. Then, his eyes lit up. "I can save ₹800 more and buy it next month!"

"That's a great idea," Arjun said proudly. "This is called *delayed gratification*. It means waiting a little longer to get something even better."

Aditya grinned. "I'll save more and get the *best* car!"

That day, Arjun realized something important—his son was not just learning about money; he was learning discipline, patience, and smart decision-making.

That night, as Aditya put his extra ₹800 into his Save Jar, he smiled to himself.

Saving was no longer something he *had* to do—it was something he *wanted* to do.

And with that, another valuable financial lesson was learned.

Avoiding Financial Mistakes

A month had passed since Aditya had started budgeting, and Arjun was impressed with how responsible his son had become with money. He had successfully saved the extra ₹800 he needed and bought the remote-controlled car he wanted.

One evening, as they sat together after dinner, Aditya excitedly showed off his toy. "Papa, I made a smart choice, right? I saved money and got something better!"

Arjun smiled and nodded. "Yes, you did. But do you know what's even more important than making good financial choices?"

Aditya tilted his head. "What?"

"*Avoiding bad financial mistakes.*"

Aditya's face turned serious. "What kind of mistakes?"

Arjun leaned back and thought for a moment. "Let me tell you a few things that many people get wrong when it comes to money."

1. Spending More Than You Earn

Arjun picked up a blank sheet of paper and drew two boxes. One was labeled **Income (Money Coming In)** and the other **Expenses (Money Going Out)**.

"Imagine you earn ₹10,000 every month," Arjun explained. "But what happens if you spend ₹12,000?"

Aditya's eyes widened. "But... I don't *have* ₹12,000! How can I spend that much?"

"That's the problem," Arjun said. "Many people spend more than they earn by borrowing money or using credit cards."

Aditya frowned. "Then what happens?"

"They get stuck in a *debt trap*," Arjun said. "They have to keep borrowing to cover their expenses, and soon, they owe more than they can pay back."

Aditya thought for a moment and nodded. "So, always spend *less* than you earn?"

"Exactly!" Arjun said. "If you follow this rule, you'll always have enough to save and invest."

2. Borrowing Money for the Wrong Reasons

Aditya suddenly remembered something. "Papa, my friend Rohan took ₹50 from me last week for snacks, but he still hasn't returned it!"

Arjun chuckled. "That's a small example of what happens when people borrow money carelessly."

He leaned in and said, "Borrowing isn't always bad. Sometimes, people take loans for important things—like buying a house or starting a business. But borrowing money for things that don't add value, like fancy gadgets or expensive clothes, can be dangerous."

Aditya thought about it. "So, we should only borrow money when it helps us make more money?"

Arjun nodded. "Smart boy! Borrowing should be a tool for growth, not a trap."

3. Never Saving for Emergencies

Arjun tapped the table and said, "Tell me, Aditya, what would happen if your remote-controlled car suddenly stopped working and needed ₹500 for repairs?"

Aditya's face fell. "I don't have that much in my Spend Jar anymore!"

Arjun smiled. "That's why people need an *emergency fund*. It's money kept aside for unexpected problems—like a sudden medical bill, a broken phone, or job loss."

Aditya nodded slowly. "So, we should always have some money saved for *just in case*?"

"Yes," Arjun said. "Even grown-ups should keep at least six months' worth of expenses in an emergency fund."

4. Impulse Buying: Buying Without Thinking

Just then, Aditya's younger sister, Ananya, ran into the room, waving a colorful magazine. "Papa! Look! There's a new Barbie set! Please, can you buy it for me?"

Arjun smiled. "But you already have three Barbie dolls."

"But this one has a *pink dress*!" Ananya pleaded.

Aditya chuckled. "That's called *impulse buying*, right, Papa?"

Arjun laughed. "Exactly! People often buy things just because they *want* them in the moment, not because they *need* them."

He turned to Ananya. "Before you buy something, ask yourself: 'Do I *really* need this, or do I just *want* it right now?'"

Ananya thought for a moment and then sighed. "Maybe I don't need it."

Arjun patted her head. "That's my girl."

5. Not Investing Early

Aditya suddenly remembered something. "Papa, you said money grows when we invest it, right?"

"Yes," Arjun said. "But many people make the mistake of delaying investments. They think, 'I'll start saving next year,' or 'I'll invest when I earn more.' But the earlier you start, the *more* your money grows."

He picked up a notebook and drew two lines. "Let's say two people, Ramesh and Suresh, start investing ₹5,000 per month. But Ramesh starts at age 25, and Suresh waits until he's 35."

"Who will have more money by the time they retire?" Arjun asked.

Aditya thought for a moment and said, "Ramesh! Because his money will grow for *more* years."

"Correct!" Arjun said. "That's the power of *compounding.* The sooner you start, the better."

The Final Lesson

Arjun leaned back and said, "So, what have you learned today?"

Aditya smiled and counted on his fingers:

- Always spend less than you earn.
- Only borrow money for important things.
- Keep an emergency fund.
- Avoid impulse buying.
- Start investing early.

Arjun nodded proudly. "If you remember these rules, you'll never struggle with money."

Aditya grinned. "I'll always be smart with my money, Papa!"

As Arjun watched his son walk away, he felt a deep sense of satisfaction.

He wasn't just raising a child.

He was raising a financially independent adult.

The Power of Giving: Teaching Charity & Social Responsibility

One Sunday morning, as Arjun sipped his tea, he saw Aditya counting the money in his jars. The Spend Jar had reduced, the Save Jar had grown, but the Give Jar remained untouched.

"Aditya, I see you're managing your money well," Arjun said, sitting beside him. "But why haven't you used anything from your Give Jar?"

Aditya looked up, confused. "Papa, I don't know what to do with it. Why should I give away my money when I can save it for something I want?"

Arjun smiled. "Let me tell you a story."

The Story of Two Rivers

"There are two rivers," Arjun began. "One is called *The River of Giving,* and the other is *The River of Taking.*

"The River of Taking only collects water. It never gives anything away. Slowly, its water turns dirty and stagnant. No one can drink from it, and no fish live in it."

Aditya wrinkled his nose. "That sounds like a terrible river!"

Arjun nodded. "But The River of Giving is different. It shares its water with farmers, animals, and people. It keeps flowing, and because of that, it remains fresh, clean, and full of life."

Aditya's eyes lit up. "So, giving makes the river… better?"

"Yes," Arjun said. "And money works the same way. If we keep everything for ourselves, it doesn't bring real happiness. But when we help others, we create something meaningful."

Finding Joy in Giving

Aditya thought about it for a moment. "But Papa, I don't have much money. How can I help others?"

Arjun smiled. "Even a little can make a difference."

He picked up his phone and showed Aditya a website. "There's an orphanage nearby that helps children who don't have parents. They need school supplies and clothes. Would you like to buy something for them?"

Aditya hesitated but then nodded. "Okay!"

They visited a stationery shop together. Aditya picked out notebooks, pencils, and crayons. At first, it was hard for him to part with the money, but when they reached the orphanage and saw the happy faces of the children, something changed inside him.

"Thank you, bhaiya!" one of the kids said, hugging him.

For the first time, Aditya felt a different kind of happiness—one that didn't come from buying toys but from making someone else happy.

As they walked back home, Aditya grinned. "Papa, I think The River of Giving feels really nice."

The Lesson from Eshwar

That evening, they visited Eshwar, who listened to Aditya's experience and smiled.

"Giving isn't just about money," Eshwar explained. "It's also about time, kindness, and knowledge."

"How?" Aditya asked.

"Imagine your friend is struggling in math, and you help him. Or if someone drops their books and you pick them up. Even smiling at someone who's having a bad day is a form of giving."

Aditya's eyes widened. "So, I don't need to be rich to help others?"

"Not at all," Eshwar said. "Some of the richest people in the world donate billions, but even the poorest can share kindness."

A Habit That Grows With You

That night, as Aditya prepared for bed, he took out ₹50 from his Give Jar and placed it in an envelope.

"What's that for?" Arjun asked.

Aditya smiled. "I don't know yet, but the next time I see someone who needs help, I'll be ready."

Arjun patted his son's head proudly. "That's the spirit."

As Aditya drifted off to sleep, Arjun sat beside him, feeling a deep sense of fulfillment.

Today, his son had learned one of life's greatest lessons—not just how to earn and save, but how to share and make the world a little better.

And in that moment, Arjun realized something profound:

Financial independence wasn't just about building wealth.

It was about using that wealth to create a meaningful life—for yourself and others.

Financial Independence for the Next Generation

One evening, Arjun sat on the balcony, watching the city lights twinkle in the distance. His mind drifted back to the lessons he had learned over the years—about saving, investing, and building wealth. But tonight, his thoughts were not about himself.

His gaze shifted to Aditya, who was sitting cross-legged on the floor, carefully arranging his money jars. His son had come a long way—from mindlessly spending pocket money on chocolates and toys to thoughtfully managing his finances.

A soft smile crossed Arjun's face. *This is how financial independence begins—not with sudden wealth, but with small, intentional steps taken early.*

A Father's Realization

As Arjun reflected on his journey, he realized something profound. He had spent years working hard, making mistakes, and learning about money. But what if he had learned these lessons as a child? How different would his life have been if someone had taught him about financial independence early on?

He sighed. "If only I had started earlier."

Eshwar's words echoed in his mind:

"The best gift you can give your children is not money—it's the knowledge of how to manage it."

Determined, Arjun decided that financial literacy would not be a one-time lesson for Aditya. It had to be a way of life.

Building Strong Foundations

Over the next few months, Arjun made financial discussions a part of their daily lives.

• When they went shopping, he involved Aditya in budgeting decisions.

• When paying bills, he explained where the money was going.

• When investing, he showed Aditya how their wealth was growing.

One day, as Arjun reviewed his stock portfolio, Aditya leaned over his shoulder.

"Papa, how does this work?" he asked, pointing at the stock market app on Arjun's phone.

Arjun smiled. "This is investing. Remember how your money grows in the Save Jar? This is like that, but on a bigger scale. Companies grow, and when we invest in them, our money grows with them."

Aditya's eyes lit up. "Can I invest too?"

Arjun chuckled. "One step at a time, champ. First, let's learn how it works."

The Next Generation of Investors

Over the next few weeks, Arjun started teaching Aditya the basics of investing in a fun, interactive way.

He created a game where Aditya could "invest" pretend money in different companies and track their performance over time.

Aditya carefully chose companies he was familiar with—his favorite chocolate brand, a gaming company, and a toy manufacturer. Every weekend, they checked the prices together.

One day, Aditya's "investment" in a toy company dropped. His face fell.

"Papa! I lost money!"

Arjun laughed. "No, you didn't. The price just went down today. It might go back up. Investing is a long-term game."

Aditya frowned. "So, I shouldn't panic?"

"Exactly. That's why we invest in strong companies and let them grow over time."

A Legacy of Knowledge

One evening, as Arjun was working on their monthly budget, Aditya sat beside him.

"Papa, when I grow up, I want to be rich. But not just for myself."

Arjun raised an eyebrow. "Oh? And what will you do with your money?"

Aditya thought for a moment. "I'll save some, invest some, and give some. Just like you taught me."

A lump formed in Arjun's throat.

This—this was financial independence. Not just earning wealth but knowing how to use it wisely. Not just securing his own future, but preparing the next generation to handle money better.

He ruffled Aditya's hair and smiled.

"You're already richer than most people, Aditya. Because you understand what money really means."

And with that, Arjun knew his job as a father wasn't just to provide for his son.

It was to ensure that Aditya never had to struggle financially—not because of the money Arjun left behind, but because of the knowledge he passed on.

Conclusion: A New Chapter Begins

As Arjun watched his son grow, he realized something important:

Financial freedom is not just about one generation breaking free from financial struggles. It's about ensuring that the next generation never falls into them in the first place.

By teaching financial literacy at an early age, he was giving Aditya a head start—a chance to build a future where money was a tool, not a burden.

And in that moment, Arjun knew:

He had achieved true financial independence—not just for himself, but for his family's future.

CHAPTER SEVENTEEN

The Final Transformation

1. The Moment of Realization

The soft hum of the ceiling fan filled Arjun's study as he sat at his desk, flipping through the pages of his financial portfolio. The neatly arranged figures on the screen reflected years of disciplined investing, strategic decision-making, and sacrifices that had finally paid off. A passive income from dividends, rental earnings, and well-performing mutual funds now comfortably covered his family's monthly expenses.

A slow smile crept across his face.

Years ago, this moment had seemed impossible. He had battled through the weight of debt, the fear of financial instability, and the uncertainty of an unpredictable job market. There were nights when he had lain awake, wondering how he would afford the future he dreamed of for his family. And yet, here he was—free.

He picked up a framed photograph from his desk. It was a picture from years ago—a younger, more stressed version of himself standing next to Suneetha and Aditya, struggling to make ends meet. He traced his fingers over the glass and whispered, "We did it."

For the first time in his life, he was truly at peace.

2. Quitting the Rat Race

The morning sun bathed the city skyline in golden hues as Arjun walked into his office, a place he had spent over a decade building his career. Today, however, was different. Today, he wasn't here to strategize for another quarter. He wasn't here to chase promotions or meet deadlines. Today, he was here to say goodbye.

With calm determination, he walked up to the HR department and handed over his resignation letter. The HR manager blinked in disbelief.

"Arjun, are you sure about this? You have a bright future here. A few more years, and you'll reach the senior leadership team."

Arjun smiled, a sense of confidence radiating from him. "I appreciate it, but I've reached where I wanted to be. It's time for a new journey."

News of his resignation spread like wildfire. His colleagues gathered around, some congratulating him, others bewildered by his decision.

"I wish I could do the same," one of them muttered, "but I have bills to pay."

"That's the difference," Arjun replied gently. "You work because you have to. I worked because I wanted to. And now, I no longer need to."

As he walked out of the office for the last time, he felt lighter, freer, as if shackles had been broken. He had quit the rat race—not because he was forced to, but because he had won.

3. Pursuing Passion Over Paychecks

For the first few weeks after quitting, Arjun allowed himself to simply *be*. He woke up without an alarm, took leisurely morning walks, and spent unhurried breakfasts with his family. There was no rush, no stress, no endless emails to check.

But soon, a new restlessness took hold—not the anxiety of financial struggles, but the urge to create something meaningful.

He thought about how Eshwar had guided him and how those lessons had transformed his life. Could he do the same for others?

The idea took root, and within months, Arjun began mentoring young investors. He conducted free workshops, sharing his knowledge with those eager to break free from financial struggles.

He also started traveling with his family—something he had always postponed due to work. Whether it was a serene retreat in the hills or an adventurous road trip, each moment was cherished.

But the most fulfilling part was the launch of his NGO, dedicated to spreading financial literacy. He knew that schools taught algebra and history, but rarely taught children how to manage money. Arjun wanted to change that.

For the first time, he wasn't chasing paychecks. He was chasing purpose.

4. A Secure & Abundant Life

One afternoon, Suneetha and Arjun sat on their balcony, sipping tea. The air was crisp, the sky painted in soft orange hues.

"Remember when we used to fight over our monthly budget?" Suneetha chuckled.

Arjun laughed. "How could I forget? Back then, even a small unexpected expense would shake us."

Now, money was no longer a source of stress. They traveled without guilt, spent on experiences rather than possessions, and invested in their children's future without hesitation.

Even their kids had developed financial wisdom. Aditya, now in college, made thoughtful money decisions. He saved before he spent, invested part of his earnings, and understood the power of compounding.

Looking at his family, Arjun realized that true financial freedom wasn't just about having money. It was about having *choices*. The choice to live without fear, to give without worry, and to enjoy without limits.

5. Sumant's Redemption: A Late but Valuable Lesson

Years had passed since Arjun last spoke to Sumant. Then one day, he received a message. *Can we meet?*

When they met, Sumant looked weary.

"I lost everything, Arjun," he admitted. "I ignored Eshwar's advice. I chased quick money, invested recklessly, and now...I'm struggling."

Arjun listened without judgment.

"I don't expect a miracle," Sumant continued. "But I want to start fresh. Can you help me?"

Arjun nodded. "It's never too late."

Together, they built a financial plan—focusing on stability over speculation, long-term investments over short-term greed. It would take time, but Sumant finally understood the importance of financial discipline.

6. The Final Conversation with Eshwar

One evening, Arjun visited Eshwar at his peaceful countryside home. The old mentor welcomed him with a warm smile.

"I've done it, Eshwar," Arjun said softly. "I'm financially free."

Eshwar's eyes gleamed with pride. "You've not just built wealth, Arjun. You've built *wisdom*."

They sat together in comfortable silence, watching the sun dip below the horizon. Arjun realized that financial freedom wasn't just about accumulating money—it was about gaining control over life.

With a deep breath, he looked ahead.

This wasn't the end of his journey.

It was the beginning of a new one.

CHAPTER EIGHTEEN

A Legacy Beyond Wealth

Arjun sat on his balcony, watching the golden hues of the sunset melt into the horizon. A gentle breeze carried the laughter of his children playing in the garden below. He closed his eyes, letting the moment sink in.

Years ago, he had been a man trapped in the cycle of earning and spending, barely able to glimpse beyond monthly bills and career ambitions. Today, he was free—not just financially, but in every sense of the word.

The journey had not been easy. He had battled doubts, faced setbacks, and even questioned if financial freedom was a myth. But step by step, with discipline and guidance from Eshwar, he had built a life where money no longer dictated his choices. Now, his investments generated more than he needed, and his days were spent doing what he loved.

Passing the Torch

One morning, Arjun found his son, Varun, sitting at the dining table, deeply engrossed in a book. Curious, he glanced at the title—*The Richest Man in Babylon.*

"You're reading this?" Arjun asked, surprised.

Varun looked up and grinned. "You always say financial knowledge is more important than school education. So I thought I'd start early."

A wave of pride washed over Arjun. He had grown up unaware of the power of financial planning, learning the hard way through trial and error. But his children would not have to. They were already grasping the principles of saving, investing, and making money work for them.

One evening, his daughter, Ananya, came running to him, holding her piggy bank. "Papa, I want to invest this in my stock account."

He chuckled. "Are you sure? You might need this for chocolates and toys."

She shook her head firmly. "No! You told me money should grow. I want it to grow."

Arjun exchanged a knowing glance with Suneetha, who smiled. Their children were learning something invaluable—not just how to earn, but how to think about wealth in a way that would serve them for a lifetime.

Eshwar's Final Words of Wisdom

Arjun made his way to Eshwar's home, a serene retreat nestled amidst greenery. He found his mentor seated in a rocking chair, gazing at the endless sky.

"You've done well, Arjun," Eshwar said without turning, as if he had sensed his arrival.

Arjun sat beside him. "I owe it all to you."

Eshwar chuckled. "No, you don't. I only showed you the door. You were the one who walked through it."

They sat in comfortable silence for a while before Arjun spoke again. "Do you think I've truly achieved financial freedom?"

Eshwar smiled. "Tell me, Arjun. What does wealth mean to you now?"

Arjun thought for a moment. "It's not about a number anymore. It's about choices. The ability to wake up every morning and decide how I want to spend my day. It's about security, peace, and giving back."

Eshwar nodded approvingly. "Then you have achieved true wealth. And now, it's time to pass it forward."

Giving Back

Inspired by Eshwar's words, Arjun launched an initiative to educate people about financial independence. Through workshops, webinars, and even a book detailing his journey, he reached thousands. His mission was clear—**to ensure that no one remained a slave to money, as he once had been.**

He started mentoring young professionals, guiding them through the maze of investments, savings, and mindful spending. The more he taught, the more he realized that financial literacy wasn't just a tool—it was a lifeline.

One day, he received an email from a woman who had attended his workshop. *"Because of your guidance, I've started my journey toward financial independence. For the first time in years, I feel hopeful about my future. Thank you."*

Arjun read the message twice, feeling a deep sense of fulfillment. Money was no longer just numbers on a screen; it was an instrument of change.

The Final Chapter of the Journey

As the years passed, Arjun's life only became richer—not just in wealth but in meaning. He traveled the world with his family, pursued his passions, and most importantly, lived on his own terms.

One evening, sitting by the fire with Suneetha, he said, "You know, years ago, I was afraid of money. Afraid of not having enough, of making mistakes, of losing it all."

She smiled. "And now?"

"Now, I respect money. But I don't fear it. Because I control it—not the other way around."

She reached for his hand. "We've come a long way."

He nodded. "And the best part? This is just the beginning. Not just for us, but for everyone we've helped along the way."

As the fire crackled, Arjun realized something profound. Financial freedom wasn't just a goal—it was a journey, one that continued long after the numbers aligned.

It was about **living life on one's own terms.** And for the first time ever, he was truly, completely free.

The End... or Just the Beginning?

Let's Stay Connected

Thank you for reading Financial Freedom Formula.

I genuinely appreciate the time you've invested in reading my work. My mission is not just to write books but to help people make better financial decisions throughout their lives.

I'd love to stay connected with you.

email me at:

ramakrishna@rkinsights.in to join in RK Insights Readers Club

When you join the RK Insights Readers Club, you'll receive:

1. Financial calculators
2. Budget and net worth templates
3. Investing checklists
4. Exclusive articles
5. Future bonus resources
6. Early access to new books and courses

If this book made a difference in your life, I'd also be grateful if you left an honest review on Amazon. Your feedback helps other readers discover the book and helps me create even better content.

I look forward to hearing from you.

Warm regards,

CMA V. K. Ramakrishna